10 MINUTE GUIDE TO

ACCESS 97

by Faithe Wempen

A Division of Macmillan Computer Publishing
201 West 103rd St., Indianapolis, Indiana 46290 USA

To Margaret

©1997 by Que® Corporation

International Standard Book Number: 0-7897-1022-6
Library of Congress Catalog Card Number: 10226-5

99 98 97   8 7 6 5 4 3

Interpretation of the printing code: the rightmost number of the first series of numbers is the year of the book's printing; the rightmost number of the second series of numbers is the number of the book's printing. For example, a printing code of 97-1 shows that the first printing of the book occurred in 1997.

Printed in the United States of America

Publisher Roland Elgey

Publishing Director Lynn Zingraft

Editorial Services Director Elizabeth Keaffaber

Managing Editor Michael Cunningham

Senior Product Development Specialist Lorna Gentry

Production Editor Tom Lamoureux

Cover Designer Dan Armstrong

Book Designer Kim Scott

Indexer Sandy Henselmeyer

Production Tricia Flodder, Daniela Raderstorf, Rowena Rappaport, Pamela Woolf

Special Thanks to Cynthia A. O'Brien for ensuring the technical accuracy of this book.

Contents

Introduction

Congratulations on choosing Microsoft Access 97! Access is one of the most powerful and flexible database management programs sold today. Whether you need a simple record of your home inventory or a complete business management system, Access can handle the job.

Although Access comes with many features to help the beginner, it's still not a simple program. You probably won't be able to dive right in without instructions. But you certainly don't want to wade through a 500-page manual to find your way around!

- You want a clear-cut, plain-English introduction to Access.

- You need to create a professional-looking, usable database—fast.

- You don't have time to study database theory.

- You need The *10 Minute Guide to Access 97.*

What Is Microsoft Access?

Microsoft Access is a Database Management System but I usually refer to it as a "database program" for short. This book covers Microsoft Access 97, the version designed for Windows 95 and Windows NT. It won't run on the 16-bit version of Windows (3.x).

Access enables you to collect, store, and arrange information as well as run reports that lead to conclusions. Here are just a few of the things you can do with Access:

- Type data directly into a database, or import it from another program.

- Sort, index, and organize the data the way you want.

- Quickly create reports and mailing labels using all or part of your data.

- Make customized data-entry forms that simplify the way beginning computer users enter new information in the database.

- Run queries that extract subsets of your data based on certain conditions.

You'll learn to do all of this and more with the help of this book.

Installing Access   If you purchased Access as part of the Microsoft Office 97 suite, you probably already installed it when you installed the suite. If you haven't installed Microsoft Access on your computer, see the inside front cover of this book for instructions.

What Is The 10 Minute Guide?

The 10 Minute Guide series is a new approach to learning computer programs. Instead of trying to cover the entire program, the 10 Minute Guide teaches you only about the features of Access that a beginner is most likely to need.

No matter what your professional demands, the *10 Minute Guide to Access 97* will help you to find and learn the main features of the program and to become productive with it quicker. You can learn this wonderfully logical and powerful program in a fraction of the time you would normally spend learning a new program.

Conventions Used in This Book

Each of the lessons in this book include step-by-step instructions for performing a specific task. The following icons will help you to identify particular types of information:

Timesaver Tips   These offer shortcuts and hints for using the program most effectively.

TIP **Access on the Web** These provide information about using Access on the Internet.

Plain English These identify new terms and definitions.

Panic Button These appear in places where new users often run into trouble.

Specific conventions in this book help you to easily find your way around Microsoft Access:

What you type appears in **bold, colored** type.

What you select appears in colored type.

Menu, Field, and Key names appear with the first letter capitalized.

TRADEMARKS

All terms mentioned in this book that are known to be trademarks have been appropriately capitalized. Que Corporation cannot attest to the accuracy of this information. Use of a term in this book should not be regarded as affecting the validity of any trademark or service mark.

WE'D LIKE TO HEAR FROM YOU

As part of our continuing effort to produce books of the highest possible quality, Que would like to hear your comments. To stay competitve, we *really* want you, as a computer book reader and user, to let us know what you like or dislike most about this book or other Que products.

You can mail comments, ideas, or suggestions for improving future editions to the address below, or send us a fax at (317) 581-4663. For the online inclined, Macmillan Computer Publishing has a forum on CompuServe (type **GO QUEBOOKS** at any prompt) through which our staff and authors are available for questions and comments. The address of our Internet site is **http://www.mcp.com/que** (World Wide Web).

In addition to exploring our forum, please feel free to contact me personally to discuss your opinions of this book: I'm **75703, 3251** on CompuServe, and I'm **lgentry@que.mcp.com** on the Internet.

Although we cannot provide general technical support, we're happy to help you resolve problems you encounter related to our books, disks, or other products. If you need such assistance, please contact our Technical Support department at 800-545-5914 ext. 3833.

To order other Que or Macmillan Computer Publishing books or products, please call our Customer Service department at 800-835-3202 ext. 666.

Thanks in advace—your comments will help us to continue publishing the best books available on computer topics in today's market.

Lorna Gentry
Product Development Specialist
Que Corporation
201 W. 103rd Street
Indianapolis, Indiana 46290
USA

WHAT IS A DATABASE?

In this lesson, you'll learn some basic database concepts and find out how Microsoft Access handles them.

WHAT ARE DATABASES GOOD FOR?

Strictly speaking, a database is any collection of information. Your local telephone book, for example, is a database, as is your Rolodex file and the card catalog at your local library. With a computerized database in Microsoft Access, you can store information, as with these three examples, but you can also do much more. For instance, if you keep a list of all your business customers in an Access database, you can:

- Print out a list of all customers who haven't bought anything in the last 60 days, along with their phone numbers, so you can call each one.

- Sort the customers by ZIP Code and print out mailing labels in that order. (Some bulk-mailing services require you to presort by ZIP Code to get the cheaper mailing rate.)

- Create a simple onscreen order entry form that even your most technically unskilled employee can use successfully.

These examples only scratch the surface. With Access, you can manipulate your data in almost any way you can dream up.

HOW ACCESS STORES YOUR DATA

In Access, the first thing you do is create a database file. That file holds everything you create for that database—not only all the data, but also the customized forms, reports, and indexes. If you have two or more businesses, you may want to create two or more separate databases (one for each business).

TABLES

The heart of each database is its tables. A table is a lot like a spreadsheet. A data table (or just "table" for short) is shown in Figure 1.1.

Each row is   Each column   The insersection of a row
a record.   is a field.   and column is a cell.

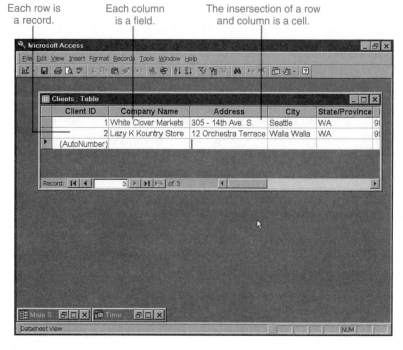

FIGURE 1.1   A typical table in Access.

Access stores each database entry (for example, each client or each inventory item) in its own row; this is a record. For example, all the information about White Clover Markets, including the Address, City, State, and ZIP Code, forms a single record (see Figure 1.1).

Each type of detail is kept in its own column: a *field*. For example, Client ID is one field, and Company Name is another. All the company names in the entire table are collectively known as the Company Name field.

At the intersection of a field and a row is the individual bit of data for that particular record; this area is a *cell*. For example, in the cell where the City column and the White Clover Markets record intersect, you'll find Seattle.

You'll learn how to create tables in Lessons 7 and 8. Each database file can have many tables. For instance, you might have a table that lists all your customers, and another table that lists information about the products you sell. A third table might keep track of your salespeople and their performance.

FORMS

All the data you enter into your database ends up in a table, for storage. You can enter information directly into a table, but it's a little bit awkward to do so. Most people find it easier to create a special on-screen form in which to enter the data. A form resembles a fill-in-the-blanks sheet that you would complete by hand, such as a job application. You'll learn how to create a form in Lesson 13.

Access links the form to the table and stores the information you put into the form in the table. For instance, in Figure 1.2, Access will store the client data I'm entering on this form in the table shown in Figure 1.1.

 TIP   **Multitable Forms** You can use a single form to enter data into several tables at once, as you'll learn in later lessons.

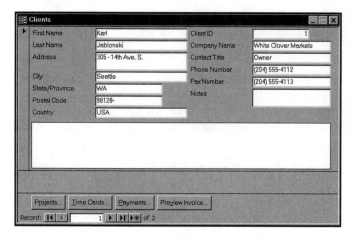

FIGURE 1.2   Forms make data entry more convenient.

REPORTS

While forms are designed to be used onscreen, reports are designed to be printed. Reports are specially formatted collections of data, organized according to your specifications. For instance, you might want to create a report of all your clients, as shown in Figure 1.3.

Print Preview   Although you create reports so that you can print them, you can also display them onscreen in Print Preview, as in Figure 1.3. You'll learn how to view and print reports in Lesson 21.

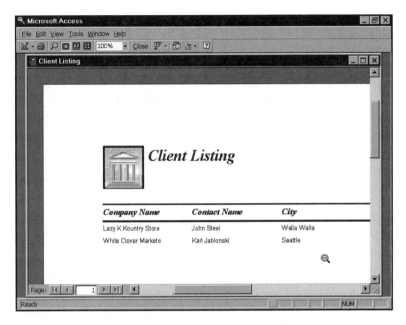

FIGURE 1.3 You can print this report and distribute it to key employees in the company.

QUERIES

A query is a way of weeding out the information you don't want to see, so you can see the information you do need more clearly. You can think of it as a sieve you dump your data into; the data you don't want falls through the holes in the sieve, leaving only the data you're interested in.

Many people are afraid of queries because of the technical terms associated with them, such as values, criteria, and masks. But there's no need to be wary, as you'll learn in Lesson 19 where you'll create and use a simple query.

HOW THE PARTS FIT TOGETHER

Even though you create tables, reports, forms, and queries in separate steps, they're all related. As I mentioned earlier, tables are the central focus of all activities—all the other objects do something to or with the table data. Reports summarize and organize the table data; forms help you enter information into the table; queries help you find information you want to use in the table. In future lessons, you'll learn how each part relates to the whole database.

ACCESS WIZARDS MAKE DATABASES EASY

Throughout this book, you will use Access's wizards. What's a wizard? It's a mini program that "interviews" you, asking you questions about what you want to accomplish. Then it takes your answers and creates the table, report, query, or whatever, according to your specifications. See a sample wizard screen in Figure 1.4.

Each time you create a new object, such as a table or a form, you have the choice of creating it "from scratch" in a Design view, or with a wizard to help you along. I recommend that all beginners use wizards as much as possible; I use them because they're so convenient. Leave the tough stuff, the Design view creations, to those with lots of leisure time.

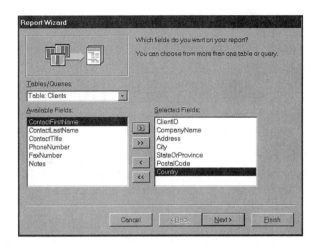

FIGURE 1.4 Wizards make it easy to create all kinds of database objects.

In this lesson, you learned some basic facts about databases and Access. In the next lesson, you will learn some strategies for planning your database. Don't skip Lesson 2! Ten minutes worth of planning now can save you hours of backtracking later.

PLANNING YOUR DATABASE

In this lesson, you'll learn some principles of good database design to help you plan your course of action.

PLANNING IS IMPORTANT!

How many times have you dived enthusiastically into a new craft or skill without really knowing what you were doing? Your first attempt was probably pretty poor, whether the pursuit was pottery or computer programming. But as you worked, you probably made notes to yourself of what you'd do differently next time, and the next time you did better.

With something as important as your database, however, you can't afford to experiment through trial and error. So in this lesson, I'll give you a crash course in the database planning that most people learn the hard way.

Before you create your database, you should ask the following questions:

- What data do I want to store, and what is the best way to organize it? This determines what tables you'll need.

- What data entry actions do I perform in the course of my business or hobby? This determines the forms you'll need.

- What information do I want to know about the status of the business or hobby? This answer will tell you what reports you'll want.

DETERMINING WHAT TABLES YOU'LL NEED

How many tables will you need? Technically, you will only need one. That's the minimum a database can function with. However, the biggest mistake most people make with Access is to put too much information in one table. Access is a relational database program; unlike more simple database programs, it's meant to handle lots of tables and create relationships among them. Figure 2.1 shows a list of tables in a database that keeps track of the employee hours spent on various projects.

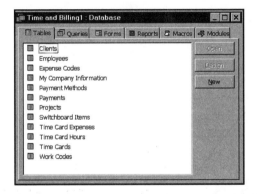

FIGURE 2.1   Access really shines when you take advantage of its capability to store many tables.

> **Plan Tables Now!**   You should plan your tables before you create your database because changing a table's structure once it's been filled with data is difficult.

Another big mistake people make is to try to make each table look like a stand-alone report. For instance, they might repeat a customer's name and address in all eight tables because they want that information readily available when it's required. This is a waste! You can easily create a report or form that includes this information whenever you need it; it needs to appear in only one table.

NORMALIZING YOUR DATABASE

When a database suffers from poor table organization, experts say it's not *normalized*. There are rules that govern how a relational database should store its tables; these are the rules of Data Normalization.

 Data Normalization   Make the tables as efficient and compact as possible to eliminate the possibility for confusion and error.

There are five normalization rules, but the latter ones are fairly complicated and used mostly by database professionals. In this lesson, I'll explain the first two normalization rules, which are all a beginner really needs to understand in order to avoid major mistakes.

 TIP   **Normalized Wizards**   Luckily, database professionals had a hand in creating Access's Database Wizard, so any tables you create using this feature (see Lesson 5) will be normalized.

1. AVOID REPEATED INFORMATION

Let's say that you want to keep contact information on your customers along with a record of each transaction they make. If you kept it all in one table, you would have to repeat the customer's full name, address, and phone number each time you entered a new transaction! It would also be a nightmare if the customer's address changed; you would have to record change every transaction.

Customer Name	Customer Address	Customer Phone	Order Date	Order Total
ABC Plumbing	201 W. 44th St.	(317) 555-2394	2/5/96	$155.90
ABC Plumbing	201 W. 44th St.	(317) 555-2394	5/14/96	$90.24
ABC Plumbing	201 W. 44th St.	(317) 555-2394	7/9/96	$224.50
Jack's Emporium	1155 Conner Ave.	(317) 555-4501	6/6/95	$1,592.99
Jack's Emporium	1155 Conner Ave.	(317) 555-4501	7/26/96	$990.41
Millie's Pizza	108 Ponting St.	(317) 554-2349	8/29/96	$39.95

A better way is to assign each customer an ID number. Include that ID number in a table that contains names and addresses; then include the same ID number as a link in a separate table that contains transactions.

Customers Table

Customer ID	Customer Name	Customer Address	Customer Phone
1	ABC Plumbing	201 W. 44th St.	(317) 555-2394
2	Jack's Emporium	1155 Conner Ave.	(317) 555-4501
3	Millie's Pizza	108 Ponting St.	(317) 554-2349

Orders Table

Customer ID	Order Date	Order Total
1	2/5/96	$155.90
1	5/14/96	$90.24
1	7/9/96	$224.50
2	6/6/95	$1,592.99
2	7/26/96	$990.41
3	8/29/96	$39.95

2. AVOID REDUNDANT DATA

Let's say you want to keep track of which employees have attended certain training classes. There are lots of employees and lots of classes. One way would be to keep it all in a single Personnel table, like this:

Employee Name	Employee Address	Employee Phone	Training Date	Class Taken	Credit Hours	Passed?
Phil Sharp	211 W. 16th St.	(317) 555-4321	5/5/96	Leadership Skills	3	Yes
Becky Rowan	40 Westfield Ct.	(317) 555-3905	5/5/96	Customer Service	2	Yes
Nick Gianti	559 Ponting St.	(317) 555-7683	6/15/96	Public Speaking	9	Yes
Martha Donato	720 E. Warren	(317) 555-2930	5/5/96	Public Speaking	9	No
Cynthia Hedges	108 Carroll St.	(317) 555-5990	6/15/96	Customer Service	2	Yes
Andrea Mayfair	3904 110th St.	(317) 555-0293	6/15/96	Leadership Skills	3	Yes

But what if an employee takes more than one class? You'd have to add a duplicate line in the table to list it, and then you have the problem described in the previous section—multiple records with virtually identical field entries. What if the only employee who has taken a certain class leaves the company? When you delete that employee's record, you delete the information about the class's credit hours, too.

A better way would be to create separate tables for Employees, Classes, and Training Done, like so:

Employee Table

Employee ID	Employee Name	Employee Address	Employee Phone
1	Phil Sharp	211 W. 16th St.	(317) 555-4321
2	Becky Rowan	40 Westfield Ct.	(317) 555-3905
3	Nick Gianti	559 Ponting St.	(317) 555-7683
4	Martha Donato	720 E. Warren	(317) 555-2930
5	Cynthia Hedges	108 Carroll St.	(317) 555-5990
6	Andrea Mayfair	3904 110th St.	(317) 555-0293

Class Table

Class ID	Class	Credits
C1	Leadership Skills	3
C2	Customer Service	2
C3	Public Speaking	9

Training Table

Employee ID	Date	Class	Passed?
1	5/5/96	C1	Yes
2	5/5/96	C2	Yes
3	6/16/96	C3	Yes
4	5/5/96	C3	No
5	6/15/96	C2	Yes
6	6/15/96	C1	Yes

SUMMARY: DESIGNING YOUR TABLES

Don't be overwhelmed by all this information about database normalization; good table organization boils down to a few simple principles:

- Each table should have a theme; for instance, Employee Contact Information or Customer Transactions. Don't try to have more than one theme per table.

- If you see that you might end up repeating data in a table in the future, plan now to split the information that will be repeated into its own table.

- If there is a list of reference information you want to preserve (such as the names and credit hours for classes), put it in its own table.

- Wherever possible, use ID numbers, as they'll help you link tables together later and help you avoid typing errors that come from entering long text strings (such as names) over and over.

WHAT FORMS WILL YOU USE?

As explained in Lesson 1, forms are data entry tools. You can arrange fields from several tables on a form and easily enter data into those fields on a single screen. For instance, a time sheet form for an employee might contain fields from the Employees, Projects, and Work Code tables. Figure 2.2 shows such a form.

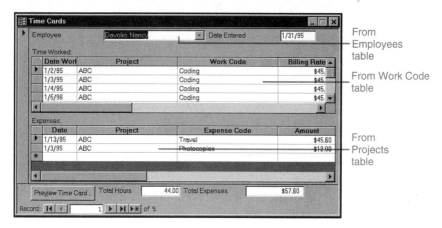

FIGURE 2.2   A form can be the link between several tables.

When thinking about what forms you'll need, the question is really "what actions will I perform?" The following list describes some actions that may require a form:

- Hiring employees (and entering their information in the database)
- Selling goods or services
- Making purchases
- Collecting the names and contact information for volunteers
- Keeping track of inventory

I Can't Predict What Forms I'll Need!   Although it's important to have effective forms, you can make changes to forms at any time fairly easily (unlike tables), so you don't have to know exactly what forms you want before you start. You'll learn to create forms in Lesson 13.

WHAT REPORTS WILL YOU WANT TO PRODUCE?

A report satisfies your need for information about your data. It's usually printed (unlike tables and forms, which are usually used on-screen). For instance, you may want a report of all people who have not paid their membership dues, or all accounts with a balance owed of more than $1,000. (You can find this information with a Query, too, as you'll learn in Lesson 19.)

A report is usually for the benefit of other people who aren't sitting with you at your computer. For instance, you might print a report to hand out to your board of directors to encourage them to keep you on as CEO. A report can pull data from many tables at once, perform calculations on the data (such as summing or averaging), and present you with neatly formatted results. Here are some things you can do with reports:

- Print a list of all your personal possessions with a replacement value over $50, for insurance purposes.

- Show a listing of all club members who have not paid their dues.

- Calculate and show the current depreciated value of all capital equipment.

- List the commissions paid to each of your top 50 salespeople in the last quarter, compared to the company-wide average.

You can create new reports at any time; you do not have to plan them before you create your database. However, if you know you will want a certain report, you might design your tables in the format that will be most effective for that report's use.

In this lesson, you planned your database tables, forms, and reports. In the next lesson, you will learn to start and exit Access.

STARTING AND EXITING ACCESS

In this lesson, you'll learn to start and exit Microsoft Access.

STARTING ACCESS

There are several ways to start Access, depending on how you've installed it. The most straightforward way is to use the Start button. Follow these steps:

1. Click the Start button. A menu appears.

2. Highlight or point to Programs. A list of your program groups appears.

3. Click on Microsoft Access. Access starts.

> **TIP** **Moving Programs Around on the Start Menu** If you would prefer to have Access in a different program group, right-click the Start button, and select Explore. Then use the Explorer to find and move the Microsoft Access shortcut to a different program group.

OTHER WAYS TO START ACCESS

Here are some other ways to start Access. Some of these require more knowledge of Windows 95 or Windows NT Workstation and Microsoft Office; if you're confused by them, stick with the primary method explained in the preceding section.

- You can create a shortcut icon for Access to sit on your desktop; you can then start Access by double-clicking the icon.

- When you're browsing files in the Windows Explorer program, you can double-click any Access data file to start Access and open that data file. Access data files have an MDB extension on them and a little icon next to them that resembles the icon next to Microsoft Access on the Programs menu.

- If you can't find Access, you can search for it. Click the Start button and select Find; then select Files or in the Named box, type **msaccess.exe**. Open the Look in list and select My Computer. Then select Find Now. When the file appears on the list below, double-click it to start Access.

When you start Access, the first thing you'll see is a dialog box prompting you to create a new database or open an existing one (see Figure 3.1). For now, click Cancel. (We won't be working with any particular database in this lesson.)

Figure 3.1   This Microsoft Access dialog box appears each time you start Access.

PARTS OF THE SCREEN

Access is much like any other Windows program: it contains menus, toolbars, a status bar, and so on. Figure 3.2 points out these landmarks. Notice that in Figure 3.2, many of the toolbar buttons are grayed out (which means you can't use them right now). There's also nothing in the work area. That's because no database file is open. The Access screen will become a much busier place in later lessons when we begin working with a database. The buttons will become available, and your database will appear in the work area.

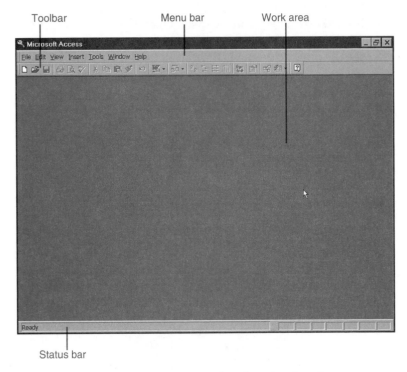

FIGURE 3.2 Access has the same interface landmarks as any Windows program.

UNDERSTANDING ACCESS TOOLBARS

If you have used Windows programs before, you are probably familiar with toolbars. They're rows of buttons that represent common commands you can issue. Toolbar buttons are often shortcuts for menu commands.

The toolbar changes depending on which object you're working with at the time (Table, Form, and so on), and what you're doing to it. More toolbars sometimes appear when you're doing special activities, such as drawing. To find out what a toolbar button does, point at it with your mouse pointer. Its name appears next to the pointer (see Figure 3.3). This feature is a ToolTip (or a ScreenTip); you can use ToolTips even when a button is unavailable (grayed out).

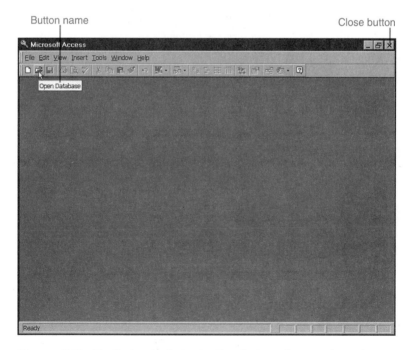

FIGURE 3.3   To find out what a toolbar button does, point at it.

Customizing Toolbars You can choose which toolbars you view at any time, and even add and remove buttons from a toolbar. Right-click any toolbar and a shortcut menu appears. You can select a toolbar for viewing from that list, or click Customize to open a dialog box where you can customize any toolbar.

EXITING ACCESS

When you finish working with Access, you should exit to free up your computer's memory for other tasks. There are several ways to exit Access:

- Press Alt+F4.

- Select File, Exit.

- Click the Access window's Close (X) button (see Figure 3.3).

Alt+F4? File, Exit? In this book, I use a kind of short-hand to tell you what keys to press and which menu commands to select. When you see "press Alt+F4," it means "hold down the Alt key on the keyboard while you press the F4 key." When you see "select File, Exit," it means "click on the word File on the menu bar, and then click on the Exit command on the menu that appears."

In this lesson, you learned to start and exit Access, and you learned about the main parts of the screen, including the toolbar buttons. In the next lesson, you will learn how to use Access's Help system.

GETTING HELP

In this lesson, you'll learn about the various types of help available to you in Access.

HELP—WHAT'S AVAILABLE?

Because every person is different, Access offers many ways to get help with the program. You can:

- Ask the Office Assistant for help.

- Get help on a particular element you see onscreen with the What's This? tool.

- Choose what you're interested in learning about from a series of Help Topics.

- If you are connected to the Internet, access the Microsoft On the Web feature to view Web pages containing help information.

ASKING THE OFFICE ASSISTANT

You have probably already met the Office Assistant; it's the paper clip character that pops up to give you advice. Don't let its whimsical appearance fool you, though; behind the Office Assistant is a very powerful Help system.

TIP

No More Answer Wizard The Office Assistant has replaced the Answer Wizard feature from Access for Windows 95.

TURNING THE OFFICE ASSISTANT ON OR OFF

By default, the Office Assistant is turned on and sits in a little box on top of whatever you're working on, as shown in Figure 4.1. You can turn it off by clicking the Close (X) button in its top right corner.

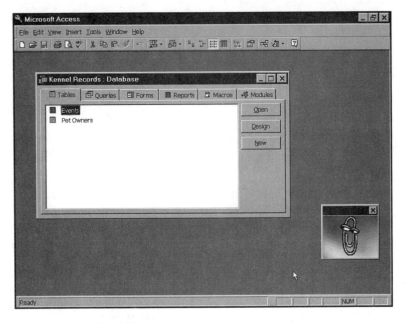

FIGURE 4.1   The Office Assistant appears in its own window on top of the Access window.

To turn the Office Assistant on again, click the Help button in the Standard toolbar or select Help, Microsoft Access Help.

TIP

Other Assistants   If you installed Microsoft Office with a Custom installation, and you chose to install the additional assistants, you can choose a different character than the paperclip. Just right-click the Office Assistant and select Assistant from the shortcut menu. Then click the Back and Next buttons to find an assistant that you prefer, and click Apply to change the character.

THE KINDS OF HELP OFFICE ASSISTANT PROVIDES

When you first turn on the Office Assistant, a bubble appears next to (or above) its box asking you what kind of help you want (see Figure 4.2). You can do any of the following:

- Type a question in the text box provided to tell the Office Assistant what kind of help you need. (More on this shortly.)

- Select one of the Office Assistant's "guesses" about what you need help with.

- Click the Tips button to get any tips that the Office Assistant can provide for the task you're performing.

- Click the Options button to customize the way the Office Assistant works.

- Click Close to close the bubble (but leave the Office Assistant onscreen).

FIGURE 4.2   Office Assistant at your service, asking what you need help with.

If you close the help bubble, you can reopen it at any time by clicking the Help button on the Standard toolbar, pressing F1, or

selecting Help, Microsoft Access Help, or clicking on the Office
Assistant window.

Extra Tips Along the Way   Sometimes you'll see a
lightbulb next to the Office Assistant. This means that the
Office Assistant has a suggestion for you regarding the
task that you're currently performing. To get the suggestion, just click the lightbulb. Click the Close button when
you're finished reading the suggestion.

ASKING THE OFFICE ASSISTANT A QUESTION

If you need helps on a particular topic, simply type a question
into the text box shown in Figure 4.2. Follow these steps:

1. If the Office Assistant's help bubble doesn't appear, click
   the Help button on the Standard toolbar.

2. Type a question into the text box. For instance, you might
   type **How do I print?** to get help saving your work.

3. Click the Search button or hit the Enter key. The Office
   Assistant provides some topics that might match what
   you're looking for. For instance, Figure 4.3 shows the
   Office Assistant's responses to the question "How do I
   print?".

FIGURE 4.3   The Office Assistant asks you to narrow down
exactly what you are trying to accomplish, so it can provide the
best help possible.

4. Click the option that best describes what you're trying to do. For instance, I'm going to choose Print a Report from Figure 4.3. A Help window appears with instructions for the specified task. If none of the options describe what you want, click the See more... arrow to view more options, or type in a different question in the text box.

The Help window that appears containing the task instructions is part of the same Help system that you can access with the Help, Contents and Index command. See "Managing Help Topics You've Located" later in this lesson for information about navigating this window.

USING THE ACCESS HELP TOPICS

A more conventional way to get help is through the Contents and Index command on the Help menu. When you open the Access Help system, move through the topics listed to find the topic you're interested in.

There are several tabs in the Help system, so you can use Help the way you want it. To access the Help system:

1. Select Help, Contents and Index.

2. Click on the tab for the type of help you want (this is further explained in the next sections).

3. Click the topic you're interested in (if there's a list), or type in your topic and press Enter.

The following sections contain specific information about each tab.

CONTENTS

The Contents tab of the Help system is a series of "books" you can open. Each book has one or more Help topics in it. Some books contain subbooks. Figure 4.4 shows a Contents screen.

To select a help topic from the Contents screen, follow these steps:

1. Select Help, Contents and Index.

2. Click the Contents tab.

3. Find the book that describes, in broad terms, what you want help with.

4. Double-click the book. A list of help topics appears below the book, as shown in Figure 4.4.

5. Double-click a help topic to display it.

6. When you finish reading a topic, click on Help Topics to go back to the main Help screen; or click the window's Close button (X) to exit from Help.

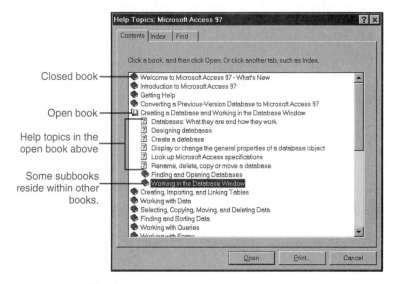

FIGURE 4.4   The Help Contents screen is a group of books that contain help information.

INDEX

The Index is an alphabetical listing of every Help topic available.

To use the index:

1. Select Help, Contents and Index.

2. Click the Index tab.

3. Type the first few letters of the topic you're looking for. The index list jumps quickly to that spot (see Figure 4.5).

4. Double-click the topic you want to see.

Type what you're looking for here.

The list jumps to match what you typed as closely as possible.

FIGURE 4.5 Browse topics alphabetically with the Index.

FIND

The Index is great if you know the name of the Help topic you're looking for, but what if you're not sure? That's where Find comes in handy. Find searches not only the titles of help topics, but their contents, and retrieves all the topics in which the word(s) you typed appear.

To use Find:

1. Select Help, Contents and Index.

2. Click the Find tab. The first time you use Find, you'll be asked to build the Find index. Click Next, and then click Finish to create the list.

3. Type the topic you're looking for in the top box (1).

4. If more than one line appear in the middle box (2), click on the one that most closely matches your interest.

5. Browse the topics that appear at the bottom (3), and click on the one that matches the help you need. See Figure 4.6.

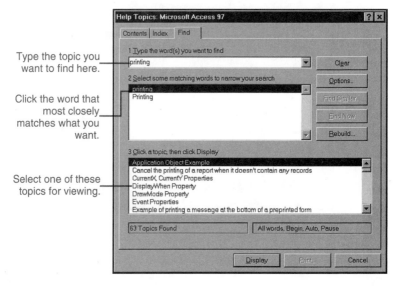

Figure 4.6   Use Find to locate all the help topics that deal with a certain subject.

6. Click the Display button or press Enter.

MANAGING HELP TOPICS YOU'VE LOCATED

No matter which of the four avenues you choose for finding a help topic (the Office Assistant, Contents, Index, or Find), you eventually end up at a Help screen like the one shown in Figure 4.7. From there, you can read the information onscreen or do any of the following:

- Click an underlined word to see a definition of it (for instance, Design view in Figure 4.7).

- Click a button to jump to another Help screen. For instance, in Figure 4.7, two >> buttons are available at the bottom of the window to take you to screens of related information.

- Print a hard copy of the information by clicking the Options button and then selecting Print Topic.

- Copy the text to the Clipboard (for pasting into a program such as Microsoft Word or Windows Notepad) by clicking the Options button and then selecting Copy.

- Return to the main Help topic that brought you to this subtopic by clicking the Back button. The Back button is not available if you are viewing a subtopic.

- Return to the main Help Topics screen by clicking the Help Topics button.

- Close the Help window by clicking the Close (X) button.

- TIP -   **Access on the Web**   New for Office 97 is built-in access to Microsoft's Web site, where you can find additional Help information. Establish your Internet connection, then select Help, Microsoft on the Web, and choose from the Web pages listed on the submenu to jump directly to one of them.

Close the Help window by clicking here.

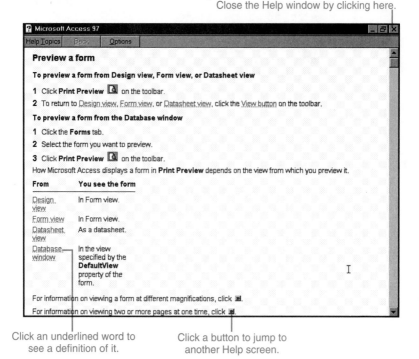

Click an underlined word to see a definition of it.   Click a button to jump to another Help screen.

Figure 4.7   Once you arrive at the information you need, you can read it on-screen, print it, or move to another Help topic.

Getting Help with Screen Elements

If you've ever wondered about the function of a particular button or tool on the screen, wonder no more. Just follow these steps:

1. Click the Help button in the toolbar.

2. Click on the screen element for which you want help. A box appears explaining the element.

In this lesson, you learned about the many ways that Access offers help. In the next lesson, you will learn to create a new database.

CREATING A NEW DATABASE

In this lesson, you'll learn how to create a blank database. You'll also learn how to create a database with pre-made tables, reports, and forms using the Database Wizard.

CHOOSING THE RIGHT WAY TO CREATE YOUR DATABASE

Before you create your database, you have an important decision to make: should you create a blank database from scratch, and then manually create all the tables, reports, and forms you'll need, or should you use a Database Wizard, which does all that for you?

Database Wizard Access comes with several Database Wizards. These are mini-programs that interview you about your needs and then create a database structure that matches them. (You will enter the actual data yourself.)

The answer depends on how well the available wizards match your needs. If there is a Database Wizard that is close to what you want, it's quickest to use it to create your database, and then modify it as needed. (Of course, you won't know what wizards are available until you open the list of them, later in this lesson.) If you're in a hurry, using a wizard can save you lots of time.

On the other hand, if you want a special-purpose database that isn't similar to any of the wizards, or if you're creating the database primarily as a training exercise for yourself, you should create the blank database.

CREATING A BLANK DATABASE

Creating a blank database is very simple, because you're just creating an outer shell at this point, without any tables, forms, etc. Just do one of the following:

If you just started Access, and the Microsoft Access dialog box is still displayed (see Figure 5.1), follow these steps:

1. Click Blank Database.

2. Click the OK button.

FIGURE 5.1   When you first start Access, you can start a new database quickly from the Microsoft Access dialog box.

If the dialog box is gone, you can't get it back until you exit from Access and restart it. But you don't need that dialog box to start a new database; at any time you can follow these steps:

1. Select File, New, or click the New button on the toolbar. The New dialog box appears (see Figure 5.2).

2. Make sure the General tab is on top, by clicking it. Double-click the Blank Database icon. The File New Database dialog box appears.

3. Type a name for your new database (preferably something descriptive) in the File name box. For example, I typed

Kennel Records. Then click Create. Access creates the new
database, as shown in Figure 5.3.

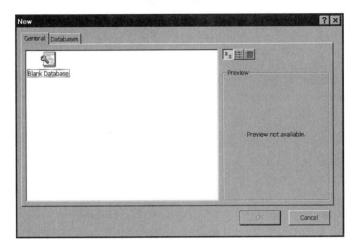

FIGURE 5.2   The New dialog box's different tabs give you options
to create different kinds of databases.

Your database is completely blank at this point. You can click on
any of the tabs in the database window (see Figure 5.3), but you
won't find anything listed on any of them. Later, you'll learn to
create tables (Lessons 7 and 8), forms (Lesson 13), queries (Lesson
19), and reports (Lesson 21) to fill these tabbed windows.

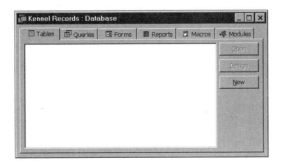

FIGURE 5.3   A new, blank database window.

CREATING A DATABASE WITH DATABASE WIZARD

A Database Wizard can create almost all the tables, forms, and reports you will ever need, automatically! The trick is choosing the right wizard to suit your purpose. Follow these steps:

1. If you just started Access, and the Microsoft Access dialog box is still on-screen, click Database Wizard, then click OK. Or, if you've already closed the dialog box, select File, New Database. Either way, the New dialog box appears.

2. Click the Databases tab to display the list of Wizards.

3. Click on one of the Database Wizards. (They're the icons with the magic wands across them.) A preview appears in the Preview area. For this example, I'll choose Contact Management.

4. When you've found the wizard you want, click OK. The File New Database dialog box appears.

5. Type a name for the database, then click Create to continue. The wizard starts, and some information appears explaining what the wizard will do.

6. Click Next to continue. A list of the tables to be created appears (see Figure 5.4). The tables appear on the left, and the selected table's fields are on the right.

7. Click on a table and examine its list of fields. Optional fields are in italics. To include an optional field, click on it to place a check mark next to it.

8. (Optional) If you are creating this database as a learning experience only, click the Yes, include sample data check box. This tells Access to enter some dummy records into the database, so you can see how they will work in the database.

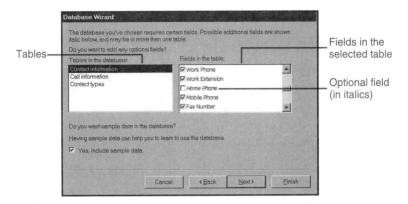

Tables

Fields in the
selected table

Optional field
(in italics)

FIGURE 5.4   These are the tables and fields that this wizard will
create automatically for you.

I Don't Want These Tables and Fields!   Sorry, that's the
price you pay for going with a prefabricated wizard. You
can't deselect any fields except the optional (italicized)
ones. But you can delete the tables and fields you don't
want later. See Lesson 9 to learn how to delete individual
fields or an entire table. If the tables and fields appear
totally inappropriate, perhaps you are using the wrong
wizard for your needs—click Cancel, and try another.

9. Click Next to continue. The wizard asks you what kind of
   screen display style you want.

10. Click on a display style in the list and examine the pre-
    view of that style that appears. When you have decided
    on a style, click on it, then click Next. The wizard asks
    you for a style for printed reports.

11. Click on a report style, and examine the preview of it.
    When you have decided on a style, click it, then click
    Next.

12. The wizard asks what title you want for the database. The title will appear on reports. It can be different from the file name. Enter a title (see Figure 5.5).

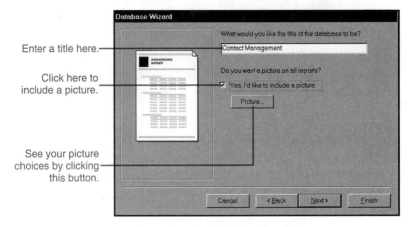

Enter a title here.

Click here to include a picture.

See your picture choices by clicking this button.

FIGURE 5.5   Enter a title for the database, and optionally, choose a graphic to use for a logo.

13. (Optional) If you want to include a picture on your forms and reports (for example, your company's logo), click the Yes, I'd like to include a picture check box. Then click the Picture button, choose a graphics file (change the drive or folder if needed), and click Open to return to the wizard.

14. Click Next to continue. Then, at the Finish screen, click Finish to open the new database. The wizard goes to work creating your database. (It may take several minutes.)

When the database is finished, the Main Switchboard window appears (see Figure 5.6). The Switchboard will open automatically whenever you open the database.

All of the databases created by a Database Wizard include the Main Switchboard. The Main Switchboard is nothing more than a fancy form with some programming built in. It lets you perform common tasks with the database by clicking a button. We won't be working with the Main Switchboard, so just click the Main Switchboard window's Close button to get rid of it.

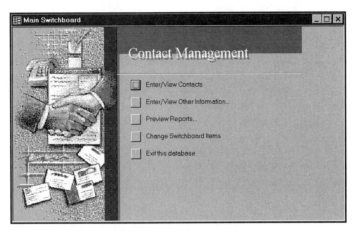

FIGURE 5.6   The Switchboard window is an extra bonus provided by the Database Wizards.

I Hate That Switchboard!   To prevent the Switchboard from opening when you open the database, select Tools, Startup. Open the Display Form drop-down list, and select [None]. Click OK.

Once you close the Switchboard window, you'll see the database window. If it's minimized, double-click its title bar (bottom left corner of the screen) to open it again. Click on the Tables tab, and you see that several tables have been created for you. Click the other tabs to see the other objects created as well.

Even though you may have all the tables, reports, and forms you need, you may still want to go through the lessons in this book in chronological order, to learn about creating and modifying these objects. If you're in a hurry to enter data, though, skip to Lesson 10, where you'll learn how to enter data in a table, or the end of Lesson 13, where you'll learn about data entry on a form.

In this lesson, you learned to create a database from scratch and using a Database Wizard. In the next lesson, you will learn how to save, close, and open a database.

SAVING, CLOSING, AND OPENING A DATABASE

In this lesson, you'll learn to save your database, close it, and reopen it. You'll also learn how to find a misplaced database file.

SAVING A DATABASE

You need to save your work so that you don't lose anything you've typed after you turn off the computer. When you created the database, you saved it by naming it. When you enter each record, Access automatically saves your work. (You'll learn to enter records in Lesson 10.) There's no need to save your work until you're ready to close your database.

When you change the structure of a table, form, or other object, however, Access will not let you close that object or close the database without confirming whether or not you want to save your changes. You'll see a dialog box like the one in Figure 6.1; just click Yes to save your changes.

FIGURE 6.1 When you make changes to an object's structure, Access asks whether it should save your changes.

Notice that the Save and Save As commands on the File menu aren't even available most of the time; they're grayed out. When you have a particular object highlighted in the Database window, such as a table, the Save As/Export command is available. You can use this command to save your table in a different format that another program (such as Excel) can read.

Using Tables in Other Programs   Another way to copy a table to another application, or to another database, is with the Copy and Paste commands. Highlight the table in the Database window and select Edit, Copy. Then open a different database or application and select Edit, Paste. A dialog box opens, giving you the options of pasting the table structure only or the structure plus its data. You can also choose to append the data to existing tables, if the fields match up.

CLOSING A DATABASE

When you finish working with a database, you should close it. When you finish using Access, just exit the program (see Lesson 3), and the database closes along with the program. However, if you want to close the database and then open another, do any of the following to close a database:

- Double-click the Control-menu icon (in the top-left corner) for the database (see Figure 6.2).
- Click the database window's Close (X) button (the top right corner).
- Select File, Close.
- Press Ctrl+F4.
- Press Ctrl+W.

Can't I Have More Than One Database Open?   Sure, you can. In fact, you may want several open, so you can transfer data between them. However, if your computer is short on memory (less than 16 megabytes), you'll find that Access runs faster when you close all files that you're not using.

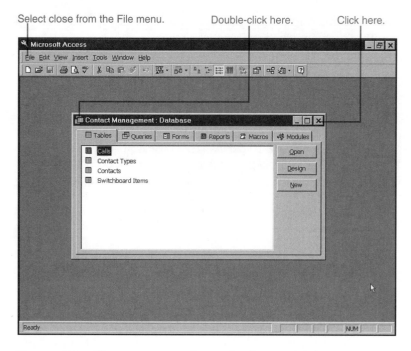

FIGURE 6.2   There are several ways to close a database.

OPENING A DATABASE

When you start Access the next time you want to use your database, you won't create a new one from scratch, of course, as you did in Lesson 5. You'll open your existing one.

The easiest way to open a database you've recently used is to select it from the File menu. Follow these steps:

1. Open the File menu. You'll see up to four databases you've recently used listed at the bottom of the menu.

2. Click on the database you want to open.

If the database you want to open isn't listed, you'll need to use the following procedure instead:

1. Select File, Open or click the Open button on the toolbar. The Open dialog box appears (see Figure 6.3)

Folder name

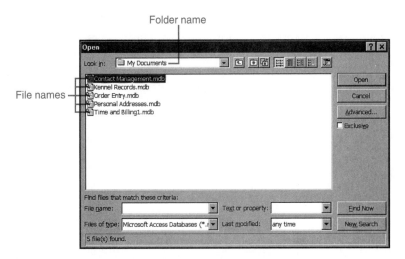

File names

FIGURE 6.3   Open a different database file with this dialog box.

2. If the file isn't in the currently displayed folder, change drives and folders. Refer to the next section, "Changing the Drive or Folder."

3. Double-click on the file to open it.

CHANGING THE DRIVE OR FOLDER

Windows 95 and Windows NT Workstation 3.51 applications provide a different dialog box for opening files than you may be used to with Windows 3.1 applications. It takes a bit of getting used to. Figure 6.3 shows the dialog box; Table 6.1 explains the buttons you see in it.

TABLE 6.1   BUTTONS AVAILABLE FOR CHANGING DRIVES AND FOLDERS IN WINDOWS 95 DIALOG BOXES

BUTTON	PURPOSE
My Documents	Shows every drive that your computer has access to, plus your Network Neighborhood and Briefcase. Use this to choose a different drive.

continues

BUTTON	PURPOSE
	Moves to the folder "above" the one shown in the Look In box (that is, the folder which the current one is inside of).
	Shows the C:\WINDOWS\ FAVORITES folder, no matter which folder was displayed before.
	Adds a shortcut to the currently displayed folder to the C:\WINDOWS\FAVORITES folder.
	Shows the folders and files in the currently displayed folder in a list.
	Shows details about each file and folder.
	Shows the properties of the selected file.
	Shows a preview (if available) of the selected file.
	Opens a shortcut menu of settings that affect the way the dialog box shows the files or that affect the selected file.

Network Neighborhood and Briefcase   These are two special locations that you may have available on the list of folders. Network Neighborhood gives you access to computers on your local area network, and Briefcase manages files between your laptop and your main computer.

FINDING A DATABASE FILE

If you're having trouble locating your file, Access can help you look. Follow these steps.

1. Select File, Open Database if the File Open dialog box is not on-screen.

2. In the File name box at the bottom of the dialog box, type the name of the file you're looking for. (Refer back to Figure 6.3.)

Wild Cards   You can use wild cards if you don't know the entire name of the file you're looking for. A ***** means "any characters" and a **?** means "any single character." For instance, if you know the file begins with P, you could use **P*.mdb** to find all Access files that begin with P.

3. (Optional) If desired, enter other search criteria:

- If you're looking for a different file type, choose it from the Files of type drop-down list.

- If you're looking for a file containing certain text, type it in the Text or property box.

- If you know when you last modified the file, choose the time interval from the Last modified drop-down list.

4. Click the Advanced button. The Advanced Find dialog box appears (see Figure 6.4).

5. In the Look in section at the bottom of the Advanced Find dialog box, narrow down the search area as much as possible:

- If you are sure the file is in a certain folder, type that folder's path in the Look in box; for example, C:\WINDOWS.

- If you are sure the file is on a certain drive, select it from the Look in drop-down list.

- If you don't know which drive contains the file, select My Computer from the Look in drop-down list.

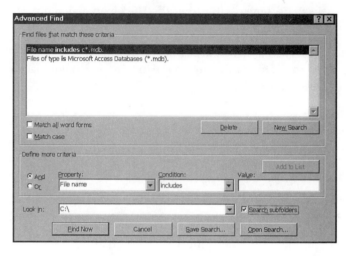

FIGURE 6.4   Use the Advanced Find dialog box to select which folders and drives to look in.

6. Make sure to select the Search Subfolders check box.

7. Click the Find Now button. The Open dialog box reappears, and the files that were found appear.

8. Double-click on the desired file to open it.

In this lesson, you learned how to save, close, and open a database. In the next lesson, you will learn how to create a table using Table Wizard.

CREATING A TABLE WITH THE TABLE WIZARD

In this lesson, you'll learn to create a table using the Table Wizard. (To learn how to create a table from scratch, see Lesson 8.)

WHY CREATE A TABLE?

Tables are the basis for the whole database. Tables hold your data. Everything else is just dress-up. If you created an empty database in Lesson 5, you'll need to create tables now, following the plan you developed in Lesson 2. If you used the Database Wizard to create your tables, you can create new tables here to augment them, or you can skip to Lesson 9, where you'll learn to modify and customize the tables.

When you create a table, you can create it "from scratch," or you can use the Table Wizard. This lesson covers the Table Wizard, and Lesson 8 covers the less-automated method.

The Table Wizard can save you lots of time by creating and formatting all the right fields for a certain purpose. Access comes with dozens of pre-made business and personal tables from which to choose. You can pick and choose among all the fields in all the pre-made tables, constructing a table that's right for your needs. Even if you can't find all the fields you need in pre-made tables, you may want to use the Table Wizard to save time, and then add the missing fields later (see Lesson 9).

Table Wizards There are three Table Wizards: the standard one, the Import Table Wizard, and the Link Table Wizard. In this lesson, we'll be working only with the standard Table Wizard.

How Can I Know Beforehand? You won't know exactly what pre-made fields Access offers until you start the Table Wizard and review the listings; if you find that there are no tables that meet your needs, you can click Cancel at any time and start creating your own table (see Lesson 8).

CREATING A TABLE USING THE TABLE WIZARD

If the fields you want to create are similar to any of Access's dozens of pre-made ones, the Table Wizard can save you a lot of time and effort. With the Table Wizard, you can copy fields from any of the dozens of sample tables.

To create a table using the Table Wizard, follow these steps:

1. Select Insert, Table from the menu bar along the top of the screen. Or in the Database window, click the Tables tab and click New. The New Table dialog box appears (see Figure 7.1).

Use the Toolbar Instead of following step 1, you can click the down arrow next to the New Object button on the toolbar. A drop-down list of the available object types appears. Select New Table from that list.

FIGURE 7.1 Decide how you want to create the new table from the New Table dialog box.

2. Click Table Wizard and click OK. The Table Wizard window appears (see Figure 7.2).

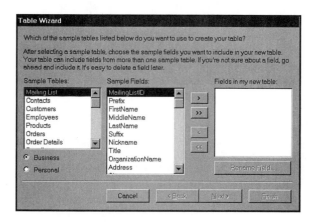

FIGURE 7.2 Choose your table's fields from those that come with any of the pre-made tables.

3. Click on a table in the Sample Tables list; its fields appear in the Sample Fields list.

- TIP - **Business or Pleasure?** There are two separate lists of tables. By default, you see the Business list. To see the Personal list, click the Personal button below the Sample Tables list (shown in Figure 7.2).

4. If you see a field that you want to include in your new table, select it from the Sample Fields list; then click the button to move it to the Fields in my new table list. To move the entire contents of the selected Sample Table to your list, click the >> button.

Name Change! If you see a field that is close to what you want, but you prefer a different name for it, first add it to your list (see steps 3 and 4). Then click the field name to select it; click the Rename Field button, type a new name, and click OK. This renames the field on your list only, not on the original.

5. Repeat steps 3 and 4 to select more fields from more sample tables until the list of fields in your new table is complete. You can remove a field from the list by clicking the < button. (You can also remove all the fields and start over by clicking the << button.) When you're finished adding fields, click Next to continue.

6. Next, you're asked for a name for the table. Type a more descriptive name to replace the default one.

7. Click Yes, set a primary key for me to have the wizard choose your primary key field, or No, I'll set the primary key to do it yourself. (If you choose Yes, skip to step 10.)

Primary Key Field The designated field for which every record must have a unique entry. This is usually an ID number, since most other fields could conceivably be the same for more than one record (for instance, two people might have the same first name).

8. A dialog box appears (see Figure 7.3) asking which field will be the primary key. Open the drop-down list and select the field.

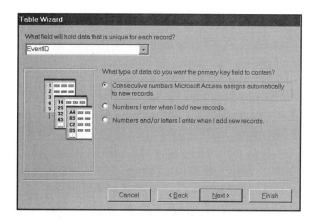

FIGURE 7.3   You can set your own primary key for the table.

9. Choose a data type for the primary key field:

   • **Consecutive numbers Microsoft Access assigns automatically to new records.** Choose this if your primary key field is a simple record number, that is, if you're numbering the records you enter consecutively as you enter them.

   • **Numbers I enter when I add new records.** Pick this to enter your own numbers. Access will not allow you to enter any letters. This choice works well for unique ID numbers such as drivers' licenses.

   • **Numbers and/or letters I enter when I add new records.** Pick this if you want to include both numbers and letters in the field. For instance, if your primary key field is a vehicle identification number for the cars in your fleet, you will need to enter both numbers and letters.

10. Click Next to continue.

11. If you already have at least one table in this database, a screen appears asking about the relationship between tables. Just click Next to move past it for now; you'll learn about relationships in Lesson 27.

12. At the Finish screen, click one of the following options:

- **Modify the table design.** This takes you into Table Design view, the same as if you had created all those fields yourself. Choose this if you have some changes you want to make to the table before you use it.

- **Enter data directly into the table.** This takes you to Table Datasheet view, where you can enter records into the rows of the table. Choose this if the table's design seems perfect to you as is.

- **Enter data into the table using a form the wizard creates for me.** This jumps you ahead a bit in this book; it leads you right into the Form Wizard covered in Lesson 13. Leave this one alone for now if you want to continue following along with the lessons in this book in order.

13. Click Finish to move where you indicated you wanted to go in step 12.

If you decide you don't want to work with this table anymore right now (no matter what you selected in step 12), just click the Close (X) button for the window that appears. (Remember, it's the X in the top right corner of the window.)

Now you have a table. In the Database window, when you click the Tables tab, you can see your table on the list (see Figure 7.4).

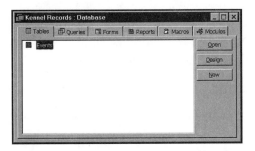

FIGURE 7.4   Now you have a table on your Tables tab.

Now What?

From here, there are a number of places you can go:

- To learn how to create a table from scratch, go on to Lesson 8, "Creating a Table Without a Wizard."

- To modify the table you just created, jump to Lesson 9, "Modifying a Table."

- To enter data into your table, skip to Lesson 10, "Entering Data Into a Table."

- To create a data entry form for easier data entry, check out Lesson 13, "Creating a Simple Form." (Don't do this yet if there are still modifications you'd like to make to your table.)

In this lesson, you learned to create a new table using the Table Wizard. In the next lesson, you will learn how to create a table without the wizard.

8 LESSON

CREATING A TABLE WITHOUT A WIZARD

In this lesson, you'll learn to create a table in Table Design view.

WHY NOT USE A WIZARD?

Access's wizards are very useful, but they do not offer as much flexibility as performing the equivalent tasks "from scratch." For instance, if you want to create a table that contains special fields not available in a wizard, you are better off creating that table in Table Design view. You'll learn to do this in this lesson.

CREATING A TABLE IN TABLE DESIGN VIEW

To create a table in Table Design view, follow these steps:

1. Select Insert, Table, or from the Database window, click the Table tab and click the New button. The New Table dialog box appears (see Figure 8.1).

FIGURE 8.1   Start your new table in Design View.

> **Quick! A New Object!** Instead of step 1, you can
> **TIP** — click the down arrow next to the New Object button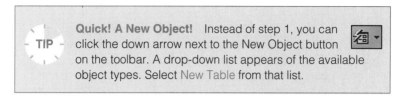
> on the toolbar. A drop-down list appears of the available
> object types. Select New Table from that list.

2. Click Design View and click OK. Table Design view opens
   (see Figure 8.2).

Start typing the first field name here.

FIGURE 8.2   From Table Design view, you can control the entire
table creation process.

3. Type a field name on the first empty line of the Field
   Name column. Then press Tab to move to the Data Type
   column.

4. When you move to the Data Type column, an arrow appears for a drop-down list there. Open the Data Type
   drop-down list and select a field type. See the section
   "Understanding Data Types and Formats" later in this
   lesson if you need help deciding which field type to use.

Field Naming Rules   Field names, and all other objects in Access for that matter, can be up to 64 characters in length and can contain spaces if you like, and any symbols except periods (.), exclamation marks (!), accent grave symbols (`), or square brackets ([]). You may want to stick with short, easy-to-remember names, however.

5. Press Tab to move to the Description column, and type a description of the field. (This is optional; the table will work fine without it.)

6. In the bottom half of the dialog box, you see Field Properties for the field type you selected (see Figure 8.3). Make any changes desired to them. See "Understanding Data Types and Formats" later in this lesson for help.

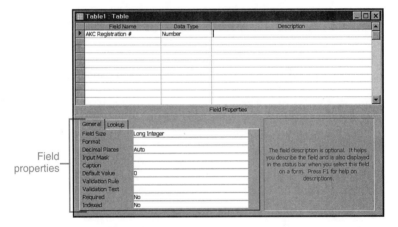

Field properties

FIGURE 8.3   Field Properties change depending on the field type.

7. If you have more fields to enter, repeat steps 3 through 6.

8. Click the Table Design window's Close (X) button.

9. When you are asked if you want to save your changes to the table, click Yes. The Save As dialog box appears.

10. Type a name for the table in the Table Name text box, and then click OK.

Switching Between Views   At any time after you've entered the first field, you can switch to Datasheet view to see how your table is going to look. Just select View, Datasheet. You may be asked to save your work before you enter Datasheet view; if so, click Yes, enter a name, and then click OK.

No Primary Key!   When you close Table Design view, you may get a message that no primary key has been assigned. See the "Setting the Primary Key" section later in this lesson to learn about this.

UNDERSTANDING DATA TYPES AND FORMATS

Each field must have a type, so Access will know how to handle its contents. Here are the types you can choose from:

Text   Plain, ordinary typing, which can include numbers, letters, and symbols. A Text field can contain up to 255 characters.

Memo   More plain, ordinary text, except you don't set a maximum field length, so you can type an almost infinite amount of text (64,000 characters).

Number   A plain, ordinary number (not currency or a date). Access won't allow any text.

Date/Time   Simply a date or a time.

Currency   A number formatted as an amount of money.

AutoNumber   Access fills in a consecutive number for each record automatically.

Yes/No   The answer to a true/false question. It can contain one of two values: Yes or No, True or False, On or Off.

OLE Object   A link to another database or file. This is an advanced feature which we won't cover in this book.

Hyperlink   A link to a location on the World Wide Web. (See Lesson 25 for more information.)

Lookup Wizard   Lets you create a list to choose a value from another table or list of values in a combo box for each record. It is an advanced feature that we won't cover here.

In addition to a field type, each field has formatting options you can set. They appear in the bottom half of the dialog box, in the Field Properties area. The formatting options change depending on the field type, and there are too many to list here, but following are some of the most important ones you'll encounter:

Field Size   The maximum number of characters a user can input in that field.

Format   A drop-down list of the available formats for that field type. You can also create custom formats.

Default Value   If a field is usually going to contain a certain value (for instance, a certain ZIP code for almost everyone), you can enter it here to save time. It will always appear in a new record, and you can type over it in the rare instances when it doesn't apply.

Decimal Places   For number fields, you can set the default number of decimal places a number will show.

Required   Choose Yes or No to tell Access whether a user should be allowed to leave this field blank when entering a new record.

Setting the Primary Key

Every table must have at least one field that has a unique value for each record. For instance, in a table of the dogs your kennel owns, you might assign an ID number to each dog, and have an ID # field in your table. Or you might choose to use each dog's AKC (American Kennel Club) registration number. This unique identifier field is known as the Primary Key field.

You must tell Access which field you are going to use as the Primary Key, so it can prevent you from accidentally entering the same value for more than one record in that field. To set a primary key, follow these steps:

1. In Table Design view, select the field that you want for the primary key.

2. Select Edit, Primary Key, or click the Primary Key button on the toolbar. A key symbol appears to the left of the field name, as shown in Figure 8.4.

Key Symbol

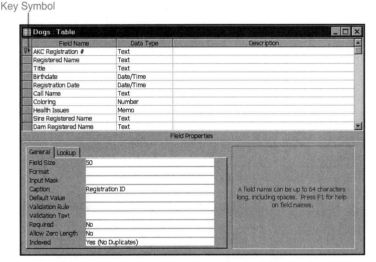

FIGURE 8.4   The primary key field is marked by a key symbol.

    Primary Key Field   The designated field for which every record must have a unique entry. This is usually an ID number, since most other fields could conceivably be the same for more than one record (for instance, two people might have the same first name).

SWITCHING BETWEEN DESIGN AND DATASHEET VIEWS

When working with tables, there are two views available: Design and Datasheet.

One easy way to switch between the views by clicking the down arrow next to the View button on the toolbar (it's the leftmost button). Then select the view you want from the drop-down list that appears.

Another way to switch between views is shown in the following steps:

1. Open the View menu.

2. Select Table Design or Datasheet, depending on which view you are currently in.

3. If you're moving from Table Design to Datasheet view, you may be asked to save your work. If so, click Yes.

4. If you're asked for a name for the table, type one and click OK.

CREATING A TABLE IN DATASHEET VIEW

Some people prefer to create their table in Datasheet view. However, Access designed Datasheet view for data entry and viewing, not for table structure changes. I do not recommend creating the table this way, since you do not have access to as many controls as you do with Table Design view.

To create a table in Datasheet view, follow these steps:

1. Select Insert, Table.

2. Click Datasheet View and click OK. A blank table opens, as shown in Figure 8.5.

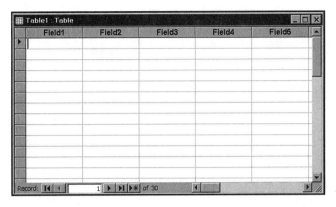

FIGURE 8.5   Creating a new table in Datasheet view gives you a quick, generic table.

How Do I Set the Field Names?   When you create a table in Datasheet view, the fields have generic names such as Field1. To change a field name, click the present name to select the column. Then select Format, Rename Column, type the new name and press Enter.

3. Make changes to the design of the table (as explained in Lesson 9, "Modifying a Table").

4. Close the table by clicking its Close (X) button. Access asks if you want to save the design changes.

5. Click Yes. Access asks for a name for the table. Type one and click OK.

In this lesson, you learned to create a table without the help of a wizard. Before you enter data into your table, you should make sure it's exactly the way you want it. In the next lesson, you will learn how to make any changes needed to your table.

9

MODIFYING A TABLE

In this lesson, you'll learn how to change your table by adding and removing fields and hiding columns.

Now that you've created a table, you may be eager to begin entering records into it. You'll learn to do that in Lesson 10. Before you begin, you should make certain that your table is structured exactly as you want it, so you won't have to backtrack later.

EDITING FIELDS AND THEIR PROPERTIES

No matter how you create your table (either with or without the Table Wizard), you can modify it using Table Design view. If you create the table without Table Wizard, Table Design view will look very familiar to you.

To enter Table Design view, do one of the following:

- From the Database window, click the Table tab, select the table you want to work with, and click the Design button.

- If the table appears in Datasheet view, select View, Table Design.

Don't forget, you can quickly change views with the View button at the far left end of the standard toolbar. Click the down arrow next to the button, and select a view from the list that appears.

Once you're in Table Design view (see Figure 9.1), you can edit any field, as you learned in Lesson 8, "Creating a Table Without a Wizard." Here is the general procedure:

Click here to see a list of different data types.

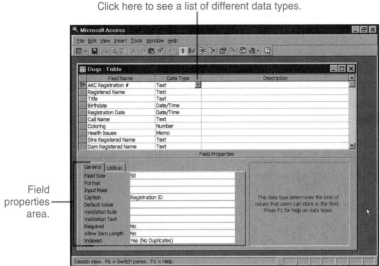

Field
properties
area.

FIGURE 9.1   In Table Design view, you can modify the attributes of any field.

1. Click any field name in the Field Name list.

2. If desired, click the field's Data Type area and select a new data type from the drop-down list.

3. In the Field Properties area (the bottom half of the Table Design screen), click any text box in order to change its value. Some text boxes have drop-down lists, which you can activate by clicking in the box.

4. Repeat steps 1–3 for each field you want to change.

I Need More Help!   For those who created their table without a wizard (Lesson 8), the above steps will be self-explanatory. However, if you used Table Wizard, you may be lost right now. Review Lesson 8 to get up-to-speed.

ADDING FIELDS

Before you enter data into your table (see Lesson 10), you should make very sure that you have included all the fields you'll need. Why? Because if you add a field later, you'll have to go back and enter a value in that field for each record that you already entered. In addition, if you change the field length, you risk truncating or invalidating data that's already been entered.

You can add a field in either Table Design or Datasheet view. Let's try it in Table Design view first, since we're already there:

1. Select the field before which you want the new field to appear.

2. Click the Insert Rows button on the toolbar, or select Insert, Row. A blank row appears in the Field Name list.

3. Enter a name, type, description, and so on for the new field. (Refer back to Lesson 8 as needed.)

DELETING FIELDS

If you realize that you don't need one or more fields that you created, now is the time to get rid of them. Otherwise, you'll needlessly enter information into each record that you will never use.

Don't Remove Important Fields!   Be very careful about deleting fields once you start entering records in your table. Once you delete a field, all the information stored for each record in that field is gone, too. The best time to experiment with deleting fields is *now*, before you enter any records.

You can erase fields in either Table Design or Datasheet view. To delete a field in Table Design view, follow these steps:

1. Switch to Table Design view if you're not already there.

2. Select a field.

3. Do any of the following:

   - Press the Delete key on your keyboard.

    - Click the Delete Rows button on the toolbar.

   - Select Edit, Delete Row.

If you prefer, you can delete the field in Datasheet view. Unlike adding fields, where there's an advantage to using Table Design view, you can accomplish a field deletion easily in either view. Follow these steps to delete a field in Datasheet view.

1. Switch to Datasheet view if you're not already there.

2. Select the entire column for the field you want to delete.

3. Select Edit, Delete Column.

HIDING A FIELD

If there's a field that you don't want to use at the moment, but will want later, you may want to hide it instead of deleting it. There are two advantages to hiding a field:

- If you have entered any records, you can preserve any data you entered into that field.

- The Field Properties you set when you created the field will remain intact, so you don't have to re-enter them later.

You must hide a field using Datasheet view; you cannot hide it using Table Design view. Follow these steps:

1. Switch to Datasheet view, if you aren't there already.

2. Select the field(s) you want to hide.

3. Select Format, Hide Columns. The columns disappear.

To unhide the column(s) later, follow these steps:

1. Select Format, Unhide Columns. The Unhide Columns
    dialog box appears (see Figure 9.2). Fields with a check
    mark beside them are unhidden; fields without a check
    mark are hidden.

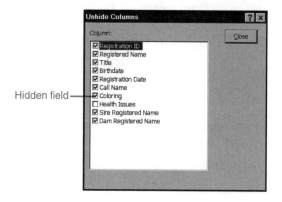

Hidden field

FIGURE 9.2   You can either unhide or hide fields with the Unhide
Columns dialog box.

2. Click on the check box of any field that you want to
    change. Clicking the box switches between hidden and
    unhidden status.

3. Click Close (X).

Hidden fields are still very much a part of your database. As proof
of that, you'll still see them in Table Design view, along with all
the other fields.

DELETING A TABLE

Now that you've created a table and worked with it a bit, you may
discover that you made so many mistakes in creating it that it
would be easier to start over. (Don't feel bad; that's what hap-
pened to me the first time.) Or you may have several tables by

now and find that you don't need all of them. Whatever the reason, it's easy to delete a table. Follow these steps:

1. From the Database window, click the Tables tab.

2. Select the table you want to delete.

3. Select Edit, Delete, or press the Delete key on your keyboard.

4. A message will appear asking if you are sure you want to do this. Click Yes.

Cut versus Delete   You can also cut a table. Cutting is different from deleting, because the table isn't gone forever; it moves to the Clipboard. From there, you can paste it into a different database, or into some other application. However, since the Clipboard holds only one item at a time, you will lose the table when you cut or copy something else to the clipboard.

In this lesson, you learned how to modify your table by adding and removing fields, hiding fields, and editing the information about each field. In the next lesson, you will begin entering data into a table.

10

ENTERING DATA INTO A TABLE

In this lesson, you'll learn how to add records to a table, how to print the table, and how to close it.

ENTERING A RECORD

At this point, you have created your table structure and you've fine-tuned it with the settings you want. It's finally time to enter records! So let's open the table and start.

TIP **Other Ways to Enter Records** Entering records directly into a table, which you'll learn to do in this lesson, is not always the best way to enter records. If you have many records to enter, it's often more efficient in the long run to take the time to create a form in which to do your data entry. You'll learn to create a form in Lesson 13.

If you read Lessons 1 and 2 (and I hope you did), you know that a record is a row in your table. It contains information about a specific person, place, event, or whatever. You enter a value for each record into each field (column) in your table.

First, you must open the table. Remember, to open a table, you double-click it in the Database window, or click it once and then click Open. Then follow these steps to enter a record.

There's a Number in the First Column! If you've set up the first field to be automatically entered (for instance, a sequentially numbered field with Autonumber), start with the second field instead.

1. Click in the first empty cell in the first empty column.

> **Cell**   The intersection of a row and a column. It's where you enter the data for a particular field for a particular record. Sometimes, the word field is used to mean the entry in a field for an individual record, but "field" really refers to the entire column. Cell is the proper name for an individual block.

2. Type the value for that field.

3. Press Tab to move to the next field and type its value.

4. Continue pressing Tab until you get to the last field. When you press Tab in the last field, the insertion point moves to the first field in the next line, where you can start a new record.

> **Insertion Point**   When you click a field, you see a blinking vertical line, called an insertion point, which tells you that is the place where anything your typing will appear.

5. Continue entering records until you've entered them all.

SOME DATA ENTRY TRICKS

You can enter all your data with nothing more than the Tab key and some typing, but here are a few keyboard tricks that will make the job easier:

- To insert the current date, press Ctrl+; (semicolon). To insert the current time, press Ctrl+: (colon).

- If you have defined a default value for a field (in Table Design view), you can insert it by pressing Ctrl+Alt+Spacebar.

- To repeat the value from the same field in the previous record, press Ctrl+' (apostrophe).

MOVING AROUND IN A TABLE

In the preceding steps, you pressed Tab to move from field to field in the table, but there are other ways to move around that you might find even more convenient. For instance, you can click in any field at any time to move the insertion point there.

There are many keyboard shortcuts for moving around in a table; they're summarized in Table 10.1.

TABLE 10.1 **TABLE MOVEMENT KEYS**

To Move To	Press
Next field	Tab
Previous field	Shift+Tab
Last field in the record	End
First field in the record	Home
Same field in the next record	Down arrow
Same field in the previous record	Up arrow
Same field in the last record	Ctrl+Down arrow
Same field in the first record	Ctrl+Up arrow
Last field in the last record	Ctrl+End
First field in the first record	Ctrl+Home

PRINTING A TABLE

Normally, you will not want to print a table—it won't look very pretty. A table is just a plain grid of rows and columns. Instead, you'll want to create and print a report that contains exactly the data you want (see Lesson 21).

However, sometimes you may want a quick printout of the raw data in the table, and in that case, follow these steps:

1. Open the table.

2. Click the Print button on the toolbar. The table prints.

> **More Printing Control**   You can set some printing options before you print if you want. Instead of clicking the Print toolbar button, select File, Print and choose your printing options from the Print dialog box. Then click OK to print.

CLOSING A TABLE

By now you have probably discovered that a table is just another window; to close it you simply click its Close button (X) or double-click its Control-menu box (see Figure 10.1).

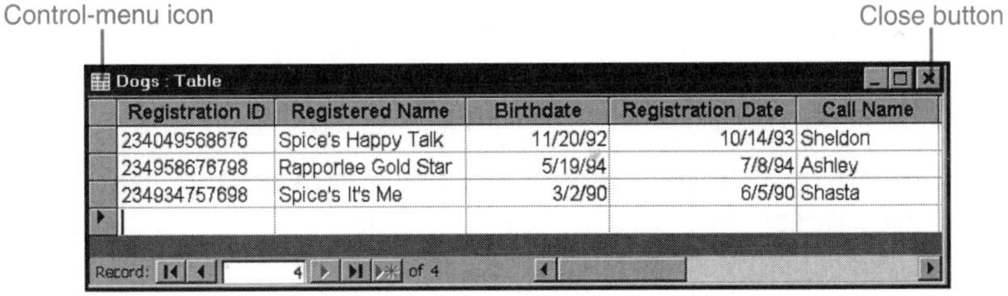

Control-menu icon   Close button

Registration ID	Registered Name	Birthdate	Registration Date	Call Name
234049568676	Spice's Happy Talk	11/20/92	10/14/93	Sheldon
234958676798	Rapporlee Gold Star	5/19/94	7/8/94	Ashley
234934757698	Spice's It's Me	3/2/90	6/5/90	Shasta

Record: 14 4   4 ▶ ▶I ▶* of 4

FIGURE 10.1   Close a table the same way you would close any window.

In this lesson, you learned to enter records into a table, to print the table, and to close it. In the next lesson, you will learn to edit your table data.

EDITING DATA IN A TABLE

In this lesson, you'll learn how to change information in a field, select records, and insert and delete records.

Very few things are done perfectly the first time around. As you're entering records into your table, you may find you need to make some changes. This lesson shows you how.

CHANGING A CELL'S CONTENT

Editing a cell's content is easy. You can either replace the old content completely or edit it. Which is better? It depends on how much you need to change; you make the call.

REPLACING A CELL'S CONTENT

If the old content is completely wrong, it's best to enter new data from scratch. To replace the old content in a field:

1. Select the cell. Do this by moving to it with the keyboard (see Table 10.1 in Lesson 10) or by clicking it.

   If you are going to select the cell by clicking it, position the mouse pointer at the left edge of the field so the mouse pointer becomes a plus sign (see Figure 11.1); then click once. That way you select the entire content.

2. Type the new data. The new data replaces the old data.

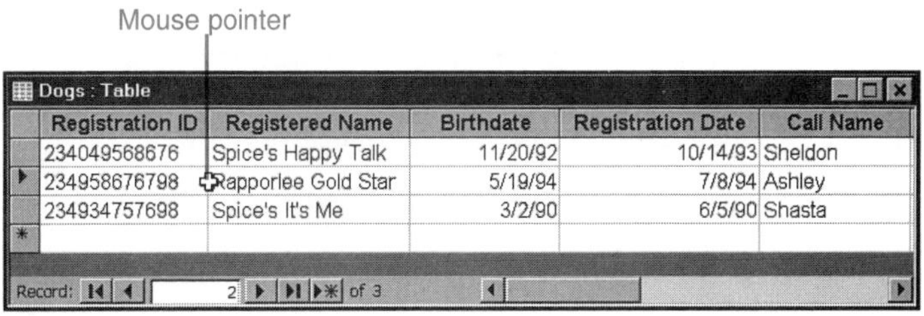

Mouse pointer
Dogs : Table
Registration ID
Registered Name
Birthdate
Registration Date
Call Name
234049568676
Spice's Happy Talk
11/20/92
10/14/93
Sheldon
234958676798
Rapporlee Gold Star
5/19/94
7/8/94
Ashley
234934757698
Spice's It's Me
3/2/90
6/5/90
Shasta
Record:
2
of 3

FIGURE 11.1 To select a field's entire content, make sure the mouse pointer is a plus sign when you click.

EDITING A CELL'S CONTENT

If you have a small change to make to a cell's content, there's no reason to completely retype it; just edit the content. Follow these steps:

1. Position the mouse pointer in the cell, so the mouse pointer looks like an I-beam (see Figure 11.2).
2. Click once. An insertion point (shown in Figure 11.2) appears in the cell.

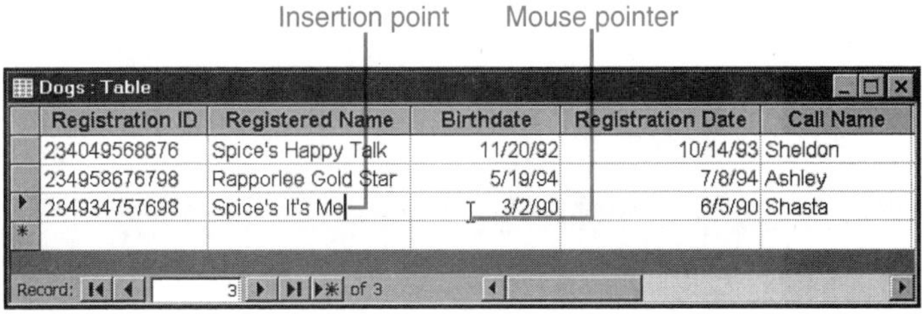

Insertion point
Mouse pointer
Dogs : Table
Registration ID
Registered Name
Birthdate
Registration Date
Call Name
234049568676
Spice's Happy Talk
11/20/92
10/14/93
Sheldon
234958676798
Rapporlee Gold Star
5/19/94
7/8/94
Ashley
234934757698
Spice's It's Me
3/2/90
6/5/90
Shasta
Record:
3
of 3

FIGURE 11.2 Click in the cell to place the insertion point in it.

3. Move to the location in the cell where you want to start editing (see Table 11.1).
4. Press Backspace to remove the character to the left of the insertion point, or press Delete to remove the character to the right of it. Then type your change.

TABLE 11.1   MOVING AROUND WITHIN A CELL

TO MOVE	PRESS
One character to the right	Right arrow
One character to the left	Left arrow
One word to the right	Ctrl+right arrow
One word to the left	Ctrl+left arrow
To the end of the line	End
To the end of the field	Ctrl+End
To the beginning of the line	Home
To the beginning of the field	Ctrl+Home

SELECTING RECORDS

In addition to editing individual cells in a record, you may want to work with an entire record. To do this, click in the gray square to the left of the record (the record selection area). The entire record appears highlighted (white letters on black), as shown in Figure 11.3.

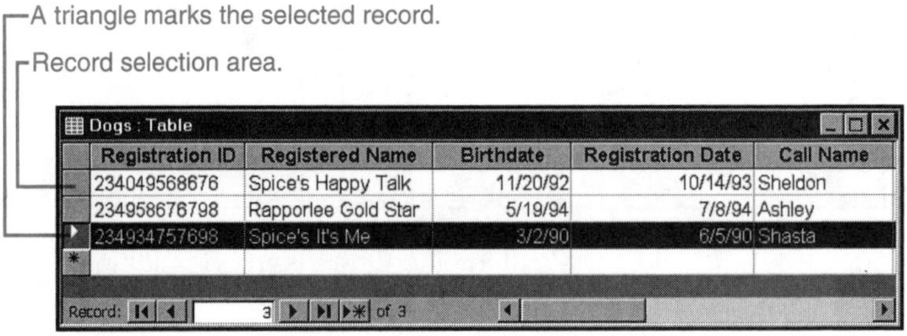

FIGURE 11.3   The highlighted selected record.

You can select several records as a group; select the first one and hold down Shift while you select the others. You can only select contiguous groups of records; you can't pick them from all over the list.

Selecting All Records   There are several quick ways to select all records at once. Click the blank box at the intersection of the row and column headings or press Ctrl+A. Or choose Edit, Select All Records from the menu bar at the top of the window.

UNDERSTANDING RECORD SELECTION SYMBOLS

When you select a record, a triangle appears in the record selection area (see Figure 11.3). There are two other symbols you might see in this area, too:

   Being entered or edited

   New Record

Only One Triangle   If you select several records, only the first one you click on will have the triangle symbol beside it. That doesn't matter, though; they're all equally selected.

INSERTING NEW RECORDS

New records are inserted automatically. When you start to type a record, a new line appears below it, waiting for another record, as you see in Figure 11.3. You can't insert new records between existing ones. You must always insert new records at the end of the table.

What If I Want the Records in a Different Order?   It's easy to sort your records in any order you like. You'll learn how to sort in Lesson 18, "Sorting and Filtering Data."

DELETING RECORDS

If you find that one or more records is out of date or doesn't belong in the table, you can easily delete it. You can even delete several records at a time. Follow these steps:

1. Select the record(s) you want to delete.

2. Do any of the following:

- Click the Delete Records button on the toolbar.
- Press the Delete key on the keyboard.
- Select Edit, Delete.
- Select Edit, Delete Record.

 Delete versus Delete Record   If you select the entire record, there's no difference between these two commands. If you don't select the entire record, though, Delete removes only the selected text, while Delete Record removes the entire record. You cannot undo a deletion, so be careful what you delete.

MOVING AND COPYING DATA

As with any Windows program, you can use the Cut, Copy, and Paste commands to copy and move data. Follow these steps:

1. Select the field(s), record(s), cell(s), or text that you want to move or copy.

2. Open the Edit menu and select Cut (to move) or Copy (to copy). Or click the Cut or Copy button on the toolbar.

3. Position the insertion point where you want to insert the cut or copied material.

4. Select Edit, Paste or click the Paste button on the toolbar.

TIP

Moving and Copying Entire Tables   You can move and copy entire objects, not just individual fields and records. From the Database window, select the table, report, query, and so on, that you want to move or copy; then execute the Cut or Copy command. Move where you want the object to go (for example, in a different database) and execute the Paste command.

In this lesson, you learned to edit data in a field, to insert and delete fields, and to copy and move data from place to place. In the next lesson, you will learn about table formatting.

12

FORMATTING A TABLE

In this lesson, you'll learn to improve the look of a table by adjusting the row and column sizes, changing the font, and choosing a different alignment.

WHY FORMAT A TABLE?

Most people don't spend a lot of time formatting Access tables, simply because they don't have to look at or print their tables. They use data entry forms (Lesson 13) to see the records on-screen and reports (Lesson 21) to print their records. The tables are merely holding tanks for raw data.

However, creating forms and reports may be more work than you want to tackle right now. For instance, if your database is very simple, consisting of one small table, you may want to add enough formatting to your table to make it look fairly attractive; then you can use it for all your viewing and printing, foregoing the fancier forms and reports.

Even if you decide later to use a form or report, you might still want to add a bit of formatting to your table, so it will be readable if you ever need to look at it.

CHANGING COLUMN WIDTH AND ROW HEIGHT

One of the most common problems with a table is that you can't see the complete contents of the fields. Fields often hold more data than will fit across a column's width, so the data in your table appears truncated, or cut off.

There are two ways to fix this problem: make the column wider, so it can display more data, or make the row taller, so it can display more than one line of data.

CHANGING COLUMN WIDTH

Access offers many different ways to adjust column width in a table, so you can choose the method you like best.

One of the easiest ways to adjust column width is to simply drag the column headings. Follow these steps:

1. Position the mouse pointer between two field names (column headings), so the mouse pointer turns into a vertical line with left- and right-pointing arrows (see Figure 12.1). You'll be adjusting the column on the left; the column on the right will move to accommodate it.

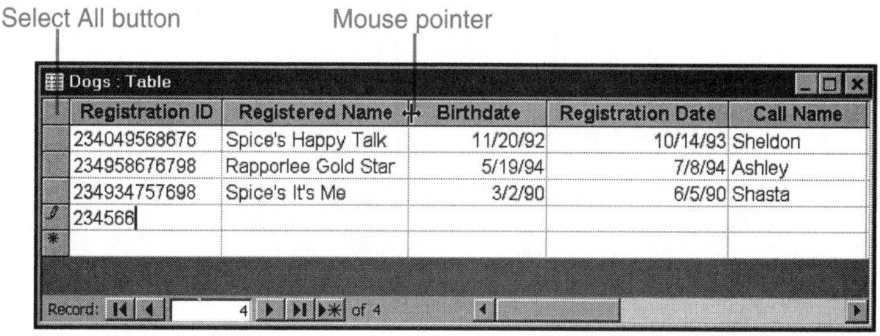

FIGURE 12.1   Position the mouse pointer between two column headings.

2. Click and hold the mouse button and drag the column to the right or left to increase or decrease the width.

3. Release the mouse button when the column is the desired width.

Another, more precise way to adjust column width is with the Column Width dialog box. Follow these steps:

1. Select the column(s) you want to adjust the width for. If you want to adjust all columns, select them all by clicking the Select All button (shown in Figure 12.1).

2. Select Format, Column Width. The Column Width dialog box appears (see Figure 12.2).

FIGURE 12.2   Adjust column width precisely here.

3. Do one of the following to set the column width:

   • Adjust the column to exactly the width needed for the longest entry in it by clicking Best Fit.

   • Set the width to a precise number of field characters by typing a value in the Column Width text box.

   • Reset the column width to its default value by selecting the Standard Width check box.

4. Click OK to apply the changes.

> **TIP**   **Column Width Shortcut**   Instead of selecting Format, Column Width, you can right-click the column and select Column Width from the shortcut menu that appears.

CHANGING ROW HEIGHT

If you don't want to make a column wider but still want to see more of its contents, you can make the rows taller.

Which Rows Should I Adjust?   It doesn't matter which row you've selected; the height you set applies to all rows. You can't adjust the height of individual rows.

One way to make rows taller is to drag one of them, just as you dragged a column in the preceding section. Position the mouse pointer between two rows in the row selection area; then drag up or down.

Another way is with the Row Height dialog box. It works the same as the Column Width dialog box except there's no Best Fit option. Right-click the column, select Row Height, then enter a new height. Alternatively, select Format, Row Height, enter the new height, and click OK.

CHANGING THE FONT

Unlike in other Access views (like Report and Form), you can't format individual fields or entries differently from the rest. You can choose a different font for the display, but it automatically applies to all the text in the table, including the column headings.

Font changes you make in Datasheet view will not appear in your reports, queries, or forms; they're for Datasheet view only.

Why Would I Change the Table Font?   You might want to make the font smaller so you can see more of the field contents on-screen without bothering to adjust column width. Or you might make the font larger so you can see the table more clearly.

To choose a different font, follow these steps:

1. Select Format, Font. The Font dialog box appears (Figure 12.3).

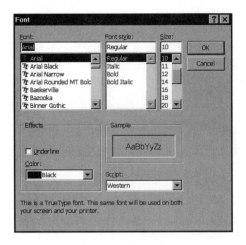

FIGURE 12.3   The Font dialog box lets you set one font for the entire table.

2. Choose a font from the Font list box.

3. Choose a style from the Font style list box.

4. Choose a size from the Size list box.

5. Choose a color from the Color drop-down list.

6. (Optional) Click the Underline check box if you want underlined text.

7. You can see a sample of your changes in the Sample area. When you're happy with the look of the sample text, click OK.

More Cell Appearance Changes   Another way you can change the look of your table is with the Cells Effects dialog box. Select Format, Cells to see it. You can change the background color, the color of the grid lines between each row and column, and whether the lines show or not.

In this lesson, you learned how to format a table. In the next lesson, you will learn how to create a simple data entry form.

CREATING A SIMPLE FORM

13

In this lesson, you'll learn to create a form, both with and without the Form Wizard.

WHY CREATE FORMS?

As you saw in Lessons 10 and 11, you can do all your data entry and editing in a table, but that may not be the best way. For one thing, unless you set your field widths very wide (see Lesson 12), you probably won't be able to see everything you type in the field. Also, if you have data you want to enter into several tables, you have to open each table individually.

A better data entry method is to create a form. With a form, you can allot as much space as needed for each field, and you can enter information into several tables at once. You can also avoid the headaches that occur when you try to figure out which record you're working with on a table; each form shows only one record at a time.

There are three ways to create a form:

- AutoForm is great when you want an extremely quick, generic form that contains all the fields in a single table.

- Form Wizard provides a compromise between speed and control; you can create a form by following a series of dialog boxes and choose which fields it will contain.

- Creating a form from scratch is the most difficult way, but it provides the most control.

Each of these is explained in this lesson.

CREATING A FORM WITH AUTOFORM

The easiest way to create a form is with AutoForm. AutoForm simply plunks the fields from a single table into a form; it's the least flexible way but it's very convenient. Follow these steps:

1. From the Database window, click the Forms tab.

2. Click the New button. The New Form dialog box appears (see Figure 13.1).

FIGURE 13.1   Choose how you want to create your form.

3. Click AutoForm: Columnar to create a columnar form (the most popular kind). This creates a form that contains your fields in a single column. Or click AutoForm: Tabular for a form that looks like a table, or AutoForm: Datasheet for a form that looks like a datasheet.

4. Open the drop-down list at the bottom of the dialog box and choose the table this form will be associated with.

5. Click OK. The form appears, ready for data entry.

If the form created by AutoForm is not what you want, delete it and try again with the Form Wizard that is explained in the next section. To delete the form, close it, and answer No when asked if you want to save your changes.

CREATING A FORM WITH FORM WIZARD

The Form Wizard offers a good compromise between the automation of AutoForm and the control of creating a form from scratch. Follow these steps to use the Form Wizard:

1. From the Database window, click the Forms tab.

2. Click the New button. The New Form dialog box appears (see Figure 13.1).

3. Click Form Wizard.

 Don't I Have to Pick a Table?   When using the Form Wizard, you don't have to choose a table from the drop-down list in the New Form dialog box because you'll choose it in step 5.

4. Click OK to begin the Form Wizard (see Figure 13.2).

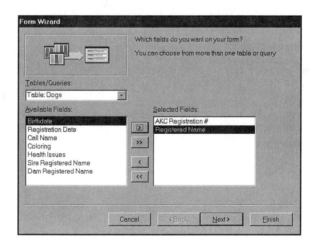

FIGURE 13.2   The Form Wizard lets you choose which fields you want to include, from as many different tables as you like.

5. Open the Tables/Queries drop-down list and choose a table or query from which to select fields.

6. Click a field in the Available Fields list that you want to include on the form, and then click the > button to move it to the Selected Fields list.

7. Repeat step 6 until you've selected all the fields you want to include from that table. If you want to include fields from another table or query, go back to Step 5 and choose another table.

 TIP **Selecting All Fields**   You can quickly move all the fields from the Available Fields list to the Selected Fields list by clicking the >> button. If you make a mistake, you can remove a field from the Selected Fields list by clicking it and clicking the < button.

8. Click Next to continue. You'll be asked to choose a layout: Columnar, Tabular, Datasheet, or Justified. Click each of the buttons to see a preview of that type. (Columnar is the most common.) Then click the one you want and click Next.

9. Next you're asked to choose a style. Click each of the styles listed to see a preview of it; click Next when you've chosen the one you want.

10. Enter a title for the form in the text box at the top of the dialog box.

11. Click the Finish button. The form appears, ready for data entry, as shown in Figure 13.3.

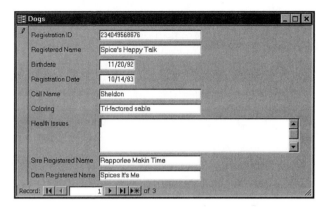

FIGURE 13.3   The Form Wizard has created this simple but usable form. The first record in the table appears in it.

CREATING A FORM FROM SCRATCH

The most powerful and difficult way to create a form is with Form Design. In Form Design view, you decide exactly where to place each field and how to format it.

The following steps initiate your use of Form Design view; you'll learn more about this view in Lesson 14.

1. From the Database window, click the Forms tab.

2. Click the New button. The New Form dialog box appears.

3. Click Design View.

4. Select a table or query from the drop-down list at the bottom of the dialog box. This is important! You won't have the opportunity to change your selection later.

5. Click OK. A Form Design screen appears, as shown in Figure 13.4. You're ready to create your form.

Only One Table Per Form   One thing you can't do with
Form Design view that you can do with Form Wizard is to
create a form containing fields from more than one table.
(At least, you can't do it in Form Design view without a lot
of maneuvering.) However, you can trick Form Design into
doing this by basing the form on a query that references
multiple tables. You'll learn about queries in Lesson 19.

In the next lesson, you'll learn to
create other areas besides Detail.

Field List button   Toolbox

Toolbox button

You can drag
the border of
the work area
down to make it
larger.

Field List

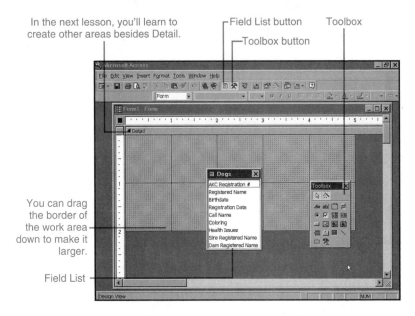

FIGURE 13.4   Form Design view presents a blank canvas on
which to design your form.

Toolbox and Field List   You'll want to use the Form
Design toolbox and the Field List shown in Figure 13.4. If
they're not visible, click the Toolbox button or the Field
List button in the toolbar.

ADDING FIELDS TO A FORM

The basic idea of the Form Design screen is simple: it's like a light table or pasteup board where you place the elements of your form. The fields you add to a form will appear in the Detail area of the form. The Detail area is the only area visible at first; you'll learn to add other areas in the next lesson.

To add a field to the form, follow these steps:

1. Display the Field List if it's not showing. Click the Field List button or select View, Field List to do so.

2. Drag a field from the Field List onto the Detail area of the form (see Figure 13.5).

3. Repeat step 2 to add as many fields as you like to the form.

Don't worry about crowded labels; you'll fix that in the next lesson.

The mouse cursor changes to show a field is being placed.

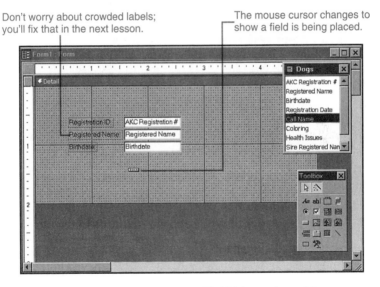

FIGURE 13.5   Drag fields from the Field List to the grid.

You can drag more than one field to the form at once. In step 2, instead of clicking on a single field and then dragging it, do one of the following before dragging:

- To select a block of fields, click the first one you want and hold down Shift while you click the last one.

- To select non-adjacent fields, hold down Ctrl as you click on each one you want.

- To select all the fields on the list, double-click the Field List title bar.

You can move objects around on a form after you've initially placed them; you'll learn how to do this in Lesson 14. Don't worry if your form doesn't look very professional at this point. In the next several lessons, you'll learn how to modify and improve your form.

Using Snap to Grid If you find it hard to align the fields neatly, select Format, Snap to Grid to place a check mark next to that command. If you want to align the fields on your own, select it again to turn it off.

If you are satisfied with your form, go ahead and close it by clicking its Close (X) button. When asked if you want to save your changes, choose Yes. Type a name for the form in the text box provided, then click OK. If, on the other hand, you want to make more modifications to your form, leave it open and skip to Lesson 14 now.

Entering Data in a Form

The whole point of creating a form is so you can enter data more easily into your tables. The form acts as an attractive "mask" that shields you from the plainness of your table. Once you create a form, follow these steps to enter data into it:

1. Open the form:

    - If your form appears in Form Design view, select View, Form to enter Form view or select Form View from the View button.

- If the form isn't open at all, click the Form tab in the Database window and double-click the form's name or click the Open button.

2. Click the field you want to begin with and type your data.

3. Press Tab to move to the next field. If you need to go back, you can press Shift+Tab to move to the previous field. When you reach the last field, pressing Tab moves you to the first field in a new, blank record.

   To move to the next record before you reach the bottom field, or to move back to previous records, click the right and left arrow buttons on the left end of the status bar at the bottom of the window.

4. Repeat steps 2 and 3 to enter all the records you like. They're saved automatically as you enter them.

 TIP **Data Entry Shortcuts** See the "Some Data Entry Tricks" section in Lesson 10 for some shortcut ideas. They work equally well in forms and tables.

In this lesson, you created a simple form and added data to it. In the next lesson, you will learn how to make changes to your form to better suit your needs.

14

MODIFYING YOUR FORM

In this lesson, you'll learn to modify a form. You can use any form, created in any of the ways you learned in Lesson 13.

This lesson is about making changes to forms. You might have a very rough form at this point, which you created from scratch, or you might have a polished, good-looking form that the Form Wizard created for you. The steps are the same no matter what you're starting with. (The examples in this lesson use a form created with Form Wizard.)

MOVING FIELDS

The most common change of a form is to move a field around. You might want to move several fields down so you can insert a new field, or you might want to just rearrange how the fields appear. From Form Design view, follow these steps:

1. Click a field's name to select it. Selection handles appear around it (see Figure 14.1). You can select several fields by holding down Shift as you click each one.

2. Position the mouse pointer so the pointer becomes a hand (see Figure 14.1). If you're moving more than one field, you can position the mouse pointer on any of the selected fields.

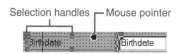

FIGURE 14.1 To move a field, first select it. Then drag it when the mouse pointer is a hand.

3. Click and hold down the left mouse button as you drag the field to a different location.

4. Release the mouse button when the field is at the desired new location.

The Label Moved Without the Field Attached! Be careful when you position your mouse pointer over the field to be moved. Make sure that the mouse pointer changes to an open hand as shown in Figure 14.1. If you position the mouse pointer over the top-left selection handle for either the label or the field, the mouse pointer changes to a hand with a pointing finger, and when you drag, the label (or the field box) moves independently. This can be handy for special situations, but it's probably not what you want right now.

ADDING TEXT

The next thing that most people want to do is add text to the form: titles, subtitles, explanatory text, and so on. Just follow these steps:

 1. If the Toolbox is not displayed, select View, Toolbox or click the Toolbox button on the toolbar.

 2. Click the Label tool in the toolbox (the one with the italicized letters *Aa* on it). The mouse pointer changes to a capital A with a plus sign next to it (see Figure 14.2).

3. Click anywhere on the form where you want to create the new text. A tiny box appears. (The box will expand to hold the text as you type.)

4. Type the text.

5. Click anywhere outside of the text's area to finish or press the Enter key.

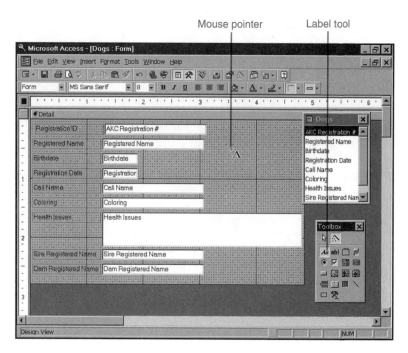

Figure 14.2   Select the Label tool in the toolbox.

 Text Dragging   Don't worry about positioning the text as you create it. You can move text in the same way that you move fields. Just click it, position the mouse pointer so the hand appears, and then drag it to where you want it to go.

Viewing Headers and Footers

You have been working with the Detail area so far, but there are other areas you can use, as shown in Figure 14.3.

To display these areas, follow these steps:

1. To view the Page Header/Footer, select View, Page Header/ Footer.

2. To view the Form Header/Footer, select View, Form Header/Footer.

3. To turn either area off, select it again.

Once you display any of these headers and footers, you can add text to them, the same way that you learned to add text in the preceding section. For instance, you might add a title for the form in the Form Header area.

Detail contains fields that will change with every record.

Form Header and Footer contain text you want repeated on each on-screen form.

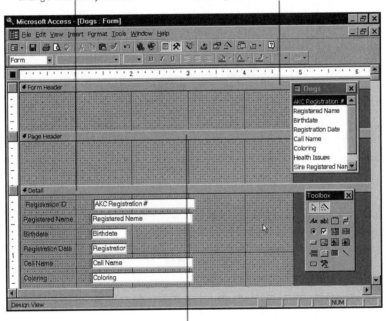

Page Header and Footer contain text you want repeated on every page when you print the form.

FIGURE 14.3   Each form can have several areas.

CHANGING FIELD LENGTHS

What if you want the Registration ID field area to be capable of displaying more characters? You just drag the field entry area to make it longer so more characters will show. Follow these steps:

1. Click the field entry area to select it. Selection handles appear around it.

2. Position the mouse pointer at the right edge of the field entry area so the mouse pointer turns into a double-headed arrow (see Figure 14.4).

3. Drag the field to its new length, then release the mouse button.

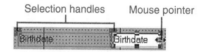

FIGURE 14.4 You can change the size of the field entry area by dragging it.

You can also resize the labels for each field the same way; position the mouse pointer at the left end of one of them, and drag until the box containing the label is the desired length.

FORMATTING TEXT ON A FORM

Once you place all your information on the form (that is, the fields you want to include and any titles or explanatory text), the next step is to make the form look more appealing.

All the formatting tools you need are on the Formatting toolbar (the second toolbar from the top in Form Design view). Table 14.1 shows the controls. To use a control, just select the element you want to format, then issue the command to apply the control.

Some controls, like the font and size, are drop-down lists. You click the down arrow next to the control, and then select from the list. Other controls are simple buttons such Bold and Italic.

Still other controls such as the coloring and border buttons are a combination of a button and a drop-down list. If you click on the button, it applies the current value. You can click the down arrow next to the button to change the value.

TABLE 14.1 CONTROLS ON THE FORMATTING TOOLBAR

BUTTON	PURPOSE
CustomerID	Lists the fields in the table you are using
Arial	Lists the available fonts
10	Lists the available sizes for the selected font
B	Toggles Bold on/off
I	Toggles Italics on/off
U	Toggles Underline on/off
	Left-aligns text
	Centers text
	Right-aligns text
	Fills the selected box with the selected color
	Colors the text in the selected box
	Colors the outline of the selected box

continues

TABLE 14.1   CONTINUED

BUTTON	PURPOSE
	Adds a border to the selected box
	Adds a special effect to the selected box

> **TIP** **Changing the Background Color**   You can change the color of the background on which the form sits, too. Just click the header for the section you want to change (for instance, **Detail**) to select the entire section. Then use the Fill/Back color control to change the color.

> **TIP** **AutoFormat**   Here's a shortcut for formatting your form. If you created the form with Form Wizard, you already saw AutoFormat at work. To see it again, select Format, AutoFormat. You'll be asked to choose from among several pre-made color and formatting schemes.

CHANGING TAB ORDER

When you enter data on a form, you press Tab to move from field to field, in the order they're shown in the form. The progression from field to field is the tab order. When you first create a form, the tab order runs from top-to-bottom.

When you move and rearrange fields, the tab order doesn't change automatically. For instance, if you had 10 fields arranged in a column, and you rearranged them so that the 10th one was at the beginning, the tab order would still show that field in 10th position, even though it's now at the top of the form. This makes it more difficult to fill in the form, so you'll want to adjust the tab order to reflect the new structure of the form.

TIP   **Tab Order Improvements**   You may want to change the tab order to be different from the obvious top-to-bottom structure, to make data entry easier. For instance, if 90 percent of the records you enter skip several fields, you may want to put those fields last in the tab order, so you can skip over them easily.

Follow these steps to adjust the tab order:

1. Select View, Tab Order. The Tab Order dialog box appears (see Figure 14.5).

2. The fields appear in their tab order. To change the order, click a field and then drag it up or down on the list.

3. To quickly set the tab order based on the fields' current positions in the form (top-to-bottom), click the Auto Order button.

4. Click OK.

FIGURE 14.5   Use the Tab Order dialog box to decide what tab order will be used on your form.

In this lesson, you learned to improve a form by moving fields, adding text, adding formatting, and adjusting the tab order. In the next lesson, you will learn about some of the fancier controls you can add to a form.

CREATING SPECIAL DATA ENTRY FIELDS ON A FORM

In this lesson, you'll learn about some special controls you can include on your forms.

As you're going to see in this lesson, it takes a little extra time to set up one of Access's special data entry fields on a form. Here are some reasons why you should do it:

- Special data entry fields make your form look more professional.

- They decrease the amount of typing you have to do when entering records.

- They decrease the possibility of typing errors, making for more reliable data.

Figure 15.1 shows the sample form you'll be working with in this lesson, with a list box and an option group already created. You can see how these controls make the form much more attractive and easy to use!

List box   Option group

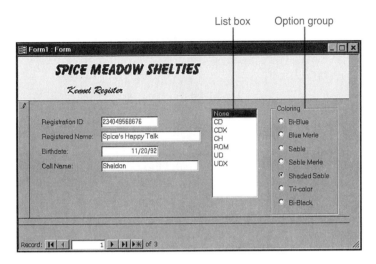

FIGURE 15.1   Special data entry controls make the difference.

WHAT KINDS OF CONTROLS?

There are several controls you can use:

- **List box**   Presents a list from which you choose an item.

- **Combo box**   Like a list box, but you can type in other entries besides those on the list.

- **Option box**   Gives you options to choose from (but you can select only one). You can use option buttons, toggle buttons, or check boxes.

Access 97 comes with a wizard for each of these control types, which makes it easy for you to create the controls.

For the benefit of advanced users, Access can create these controls either with or without the wizards. To make sure that Access knows you want to use wizards, make sure you select the Wizards button in the Toolbox (see Figure 15.2). Since creating custom controls without a wizard is rather difficult, this lesson will focus on the wizards.

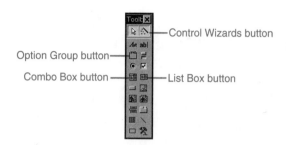

Control Wizards button

Option Group button

Combo Box button

List Box button

FIGURE 15.2   To use wizards, select the Control Wizards button.

CREATING A LIST BOX OR COMBO BOX

A list box or combo box can come in handy if there are certain values that you find yourself typing repeatedly into a field. For example, if you have to enter the name of one of your 12 branch offices each time you use a form, you might find it easier to create a list box containing the branch office names, and then you can simply click to select from the list. With a list box, the person doing the data entry is limited to the pre-typed choices that display.

A combo box is useful when a list box is appropriate, but there's a possibility that a different entry might occasionally be needed. For example, if most of your customers come from one of six states, but occasionally you get a new customer from another state, you might use a combo box. During data entry, you could choose the state from the list when appropriate and type a new state when it's not.

Follow these steps to create a list box or combo box from Form Design view:

1. Make sure that the Control Wizards button in the toolbox is selected.

2. Click the List Box or Combo Box button in the toolbox (see Figure 15.2). The mouse pointer changes to show the type of box you selected.

3. Drag your mouse to draw a box on the grid where you want the new element to be. When you release the mouse button, the wizard starts.

4. On the first screen of the wizard, click the button labeled I will type the values that I want. Then click Next.

Another Way to Enter Values If you prefer, you can **TIP** create a separate table beforehand containing the values you want to use in this field, and then select I want the list box to look up the values in a table or query. You'll then choose which table or query instead of typing in the values.

5. Next, you'll be asked to type in the values that you want to appear in the list. Type them in (as shown in Figure 15.3), pressing the Tab key after each one. Then click Next.

One column is usually sufficient.   You can drag here to change the column width.

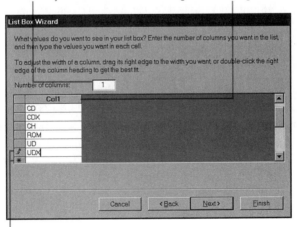

These are the same symbols as when you enter records.

FIGURE 15.3   Type the values that you want to choose from in this list or combo box.

6. Select Store the value in this field, and choose which field should receive the data. For example, I'm entering the various titles a dog can earn in dog shows, so I'll select the Title field here and click **Next**.

7. Type the title that you want to appear for the element (that is, the field label).

8. Click Finish. Your new box appears, with the name of the field you chose in step 6 in the box.

Where Are My Values?   Don't be alarmed that the values you entered for the field don't appear in the box. You'll see them in Form view. You can switch to Form view to see them now if you want to be sure; switch back to Form Design view when you finish looking.

I Picked the Wrong Type!   You can easily switch between a list box and a combo box, even after you've created it. In Form Design view, right-click on the box, click Change to and select a new box type.

CREATING AN OPTION GROUP

An option group is helpful if you have a few choices for a field entry and you never enter anything but those few choices. For instance, if you're recording the results of a multiple-choice quiz, the answer to question 5 is always A, B, C, or D—never anything else.

What About "Other" As a Quiz Answer?   If you have a questionnaire in which the respondent can choose A, B, C, or D, or enter his or her own response under "Other," you're better off using a combo box on your form, because a combo box allows for new entries.

An option group can include toggle buttons, option buttons, or check boxes. These are simply different styles; they all do the same thing. You can select only one of the choices shown in an option group. When you select another, the one you originally selected is deselected.

That's Not How Check Boxes Usually Work!   You're right. In almost all Windows programs, check boxes are nonexclusive. You can select as many of them in a group as you like. But in this case, they aren't real check boxes; they're just option buttons that you can style to look like check boxes or toggle buttons if you want.

To create an option group, follow these steps:

1. Make sure that the Control Wizards button in the toolbox is selected.

2. Click the Option Group button in the toolbox (refer to Figure 15.2). Your mouse pointer changes to show the Option Group icon.

3. Drag your mouse pointer on your form to draw a box where you want the option group to appear. When you release the mouse button, the wizard starts.

4. First, you're asked to enter the values you want for each button (see Figure 15.4). Do so, pressing Tab after each one; then click Next.

5. Choose Yes or No when asked if you want a default choice. If you choose Yes, select the default choice from the drop-down list. (This is the choice that will appear automatically when you use the form.) Then click Next.

6. When asked what value you want to assign to each option, click Next to continue. You don't need to change the assigned default values.

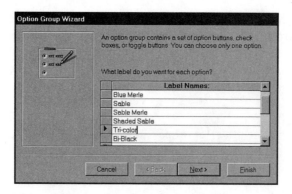

FIGURE 15.4   Enter the labels you want for each option here.

7. Click Store the value in this field, and choose which field should receive the data from the drop-down list. For instance, I'm entering the various colors a Shetland Sheepdog can be, so I'll select the Coloring field here and click Next.

8. Click to select a type of control (option button, check box, or toggle button), and a style for the controls; then click Next.

9. Enter a caption for the option group (in this example, you would use **Coloring**). Then click Finish. You have created your group.

They're All Marked!   When you're in Form Design view, each option in an option group is selected, just to show that it can be. When you are actually using the form, however (in Form view), only one option in the group can be selected at a time. If you do not select a default option (step 5), all of them will be gray (neither selected nor unselected) for a record until you choose one.

In this lesson, you learned to create list and combo boxes and option groups on your forms. In the next lesson, you will learn how to further improve the look of a form by adding graphics to it.

ADDING GRAPHICS TO FORMS

In this lesson, you'll learn how to improve the look of a form by adding graphics to it.

It's not just an old cliche: A picture is worth a thousand words. Graphics do make a difference. Using clip art and other pictures and graphics on your Access form can make your form look more professional and more polished.

There are several kinds of graphics you can include in a form. You can import a piece of clip art that comes with Microsoft Office and you can import pictures from other programs (in a variety of formats). Or, using Windows Paint program, you can draw a picture yourself.

Clip Art Pre-drawn "generic" images that you can put to use in your computerized databases, documents, spreadsheets, and so on. Clip art is not copyrighted, so you can use it without paying royalties or getting permission.

If you are used to other Microsoft Office programs like Word and PowerPoint, you may be disappointed to learn that Microsoft Access does not use the ClipArt Gallery 3.0 program that the others do.

You should also know that Microsoft Access, when purchased as a stand-alone product, does not come with any clip art. If you bought Access as part of the Microsoft Office package, you have a Clipart folder in your MSOffice folder, but it doesn't have anything to do with your Access installation per se. You can use that clip art in Access as you would any other picture, however.

TIP

A Back Door Into Clip Art   If you have other Office programs installed, you also have the Clip Gallery 3.0 program, which catalogs and controls clip art. You can access it by following the steps in this section and selecting Microsoft Clip Gallery as the Object Type. The Clip Gallery opens and you can select clip art from it. However, clip art inserted in this way is not resizable, so it is of limited usefulness.

IMPORTING A GRAPHIC

Access lets you place a graphic on a form, just like it lets you place any other object on a form (like a field or a line of text, for instance). Once you place the graphic, you can move it around the same as any other object, too. To place a graphic on a form, follow these steps:

1. Display the form in Form Design view.

2. Select Insert, Picture. The Insert Picture dialog box appears (see Figure 16.1).

Change to the drive and folder containing the picture you want to use.

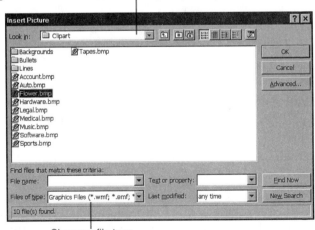

Choose a file type.

FIGURE 16.1   Choose the picture you want to import from this dialog box.

3. If you want to see only a certain file type on the list, open the Files of type drop-down list at the bottom of the dialog box, and choose the file type you want. By default, Graphics Files appears there, which includes all types of graphics files on the list, including clip art, bitmap files (created with Windows Paint program), and more.

4. Change the drive or folder if necessary to locate the graphic file you want. (See Lesson 6 if you need help navigating the drives and folders.)

5. (Optional) If you are not sure which file you want, click the Preview button in the dialog box. The view changes to show the currently highlighted file (see Figure 16.2). Click various files on the list to preview them before you make your selection.

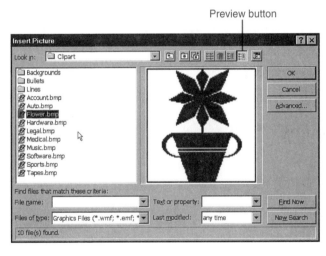

FIGURE 16.2   You can preview graphics before you import them.

6. When you've found the graphic you want to import, click OK. It appears on your form.

7. Drag the graphic to the desired location.

8. If desired, resize the graphic by dragging one of its selection handles (see Figure 16.3).

> **My Picture Is Changing Shape!** Hold down the Shift
> key while dragging to maintain the aspect ratio (the ratio
> of height-to-width). If you don't hold down Shift, Access
> allows you to squash or elongate the picture as you
> resize.

These grey squares are selection handles.

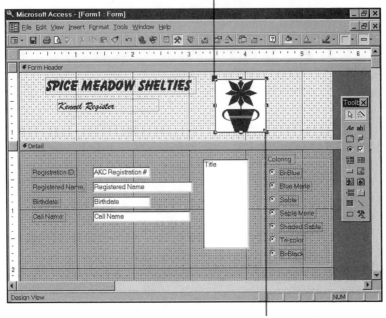

The mouse pointer changes to a double arrow
when positioned over a selection handle.

FIGURE 16.3   Drag a selection handle to resize a graphic.

CREATING A NEW PICTURE

Another way to get a graphic onto your form is to draw it yourself. You can use Windows Paint program to create a simple drawing without leaving Access.

Paint A simple art program that comes with Windows 95 and Windows NT versions 3.51 and higher. You can use it to make simple drawings, but it's not sophisticated enough to create professional-quality artwork. Try a program like CorelDRAW or Freehand if you need to create higher-quality art.

To use Paint, follow these steps:

1. Open the form in Form Design view.

2. Select Insert, Object. The Insert Object dialog box appears.

3. Click the Create New option. A list of programs appears.

4. Find Bitmap Image on the list, and click it (see Figure 16.4). Click OK and a blank Paint screen appears, as shown in Figure 16.5.

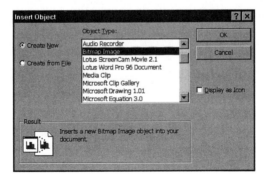

FIGURE 16.4   Use this dialog box to start a new Paint picture.

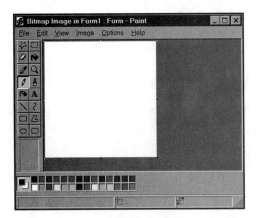

FIGURE 16.5   Use Paint to create a picture.

5. Use the Paint tools (as described in your Windows documentation) to create your drawing.

6. From Paint, select File, Exit and press Enter.

7. If you want to edit the drawing (including resizing), double-click it to re-enter Paint.

In this lesson, you learned how to import pictures into an Access form, and how to use Paint from within Access to create a picture. You'll see that these skills will also apply to reports when you learn to create those in Lesson 21. In the next lesson, you will learn how to search for data in an Access database.

Searching for Data

In this lesson, you'll learn the most basic ways to search for data in a database using the Find and Replace features.

Using the Find Feature

The Find feature is useful for locating a particular record that you have previously entered. For instance, if you keep a database of customers, you might want to find a particular customer's record quickly when he is ready to make a purchase, so you can verify his address. Or, to continue the Kennel example we've been using, you could quickly find the record for the dog with the call name of Sheldon, to look up his birth date.

>
> **TIP** **Finding More Than One Record** If you need to find several records at once, Find is not the best tool. It only finds one record at a time. A better tool for finding multiple records is a filter, discussed in Lesson 18.

To find a particular record, follow these steps:

1. Switch to either Datasheet view or Form view. Either one supports the Find feature.

2. Click in the field that contains the data you want to find, if you know which field it is. For instance, if you're going to look for a customer based on his last name, click in the **Name** field.

3. Click the Find tool in the toolbar, select Edit, Find or press Ctrl+F. The Find dialog box appears (see Figure 17.1).

Figure 17.1   Use the Find dialog box to find data in a record.

4. Type the text or numbers that you want to find into the **Find What** text box.

5. Open the Match drop-down list and select one of the following:

   Whole Field   Finds fields where the specified text is the only thing in that field. For instance, "Smith" would not find "Smithsonian."

   Start of Field   Finds fields that begin with the specified text. For instance, "Smith" would find "Smith" and "Smithsonian," but not "Joe Smith."

   Any Part of Field   Finds fields that contain the specified text in any way. "Smith" would find "Smith," "Smithsonian," and "Joe Smith."

6. If you want to search only forward from the current record, open the Search drop-down list and select Down. If you want to search only backward, select Up. The default is All, which searches all records.

7. To limit the match to only entries that are the same case (upper or lower), select the Match Case check box. After doing this, "Smith" would not find "SMITH" or "smith."

8. To find only fields with the same formatting as the text you type, select Search Fields as Formatted. With this option on, "12/12/95" would not find "12-12-95," even though they are the same date, because they're formatted differently. **The Search Fields as Formatted** option is available only if you select Search Only Current Field (see step 9).

> **Don't Slow Down** Don't use the Search Fields as For-
> matted option unless you specifically need it, because it
> makes your search go more slowly.

TIP

9. To limit the search to the field where you clicked when
   you started this procedure, select the Search Only Current
   Field check box. (Do this whenever possible, because it
   makes the search faster.) If you don't know what field the
   data is in, leave this unmarked.

10. Click Find First to find the first match for your search.

11. If needed, move the Find dialog box out of the way by
    dragging its title bar so you can see the record it found.
    Access highlights the field entry containing the found
    text (see Figure 17.2).

When the Search Only Current Field option is on, the   Access highlights
title bar shows which field is being searched.   the found text.

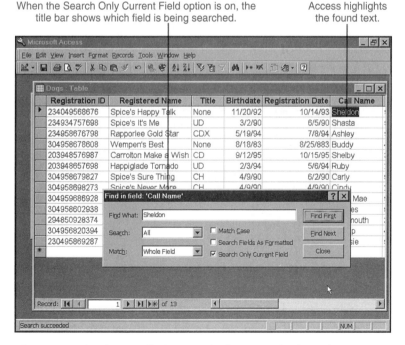

FIGURE 17.2 Access finds records that contain the selected text,
one instance at a time.

12. To find the next occurrence, click Find Next. If Access cannot find any more occurrences, it tells you the search item was not found. Click OK to clear that message.

13. When you finish finding your data, click Close to close the Find dialog box.

Using the Replace Feature

Replacing is a lot like finding; it finds the specified text. But as an extra bonus, it replaces the found text with text that you specify. For instance, if you found that you misspelled a brand name in your inventory you could replace the word with the correct spelling. Or, in our dog kennel example, you could find the dog named Sheldon and change his name to Sherman, if his new owners changed his name.

To find and replace data, follow these steps:

1. Select Edit, Replace or press Ctrl+H. The Replace dialog box appears (see figure 17.3).

2. Type the text you want to find in the **Find What** text box.

3. Type the text you want to replace it with in the **Replace With** text box.

4. Select any options you want, as you learned to do with the Find dialog box in the previous section.

There's No Match   Compared to the Find dialog box, the one thing that the Replace dialog box lacks is the Match drop-down list. The Replace feature always uses the **Any Part of Field** option for matching.

5. Click Find Next. Access finds the first occurrence of the text.

6. If needed, drag the title bar of the Replace dialog box to move the box so you can see the text that was found.

7. Click the Replace button to replace the text.

Type the text   Type the text you   Click here when
you want to find   want to replace it   you're ready to start
here.   with here.   the search.

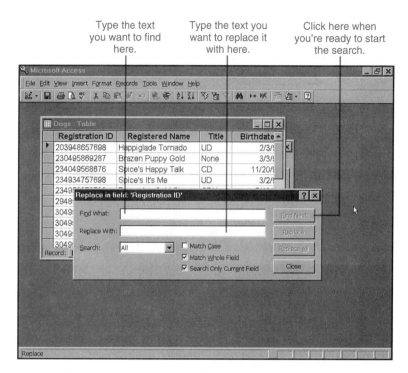

FIGURE 17.3   You can find specific text and replace it with different text.

8. Click Find Next to find other occurrences if desired, and replace them by clicking the Replace button.

Replace All   If you are certain you want to replace every instance of the text in the entire table, click Replace All. It's quicker than alternating repeatedly between Find Next and Replace. Be careful, though! You may not realize all the instances that may be changed—for instance, you wouldn't want to change "will" to "would" only to find that "willfully" has been changed to "wouldfully."

9. When you finish replacing, click Close.

OTHER WAYS TO FIND DATA

The Find and Replace features work well on individual records, but there are several more sophisticated ways of locating data in your database, as you'll learn in upcoming lessons. They include:

- **Sorting**—Rearranging the data on-screen so it's easier to skim through the list to find what you want. See Lesson 18.

- **Filtering**—Narrowing down the list to eliminate the data you know you don't want to see. See Lesson 18.

- **Indexing**—Defining other fields besides the primary key that you want Access to keep track of (that is, keep an index of). Indexing is optional, but in large databases it makes your searching and sorting faster. See Lesson 18.

- **Querying**—Creating a more formal filter with complex criteria that you can save and apply again and again. See Lessons 19–20.

- **Reporting**—Creating a printed report containing only the records and fields that you're interested in. See Lessons 21–22.

In this lesson, you learned to find and replace data in a database. In the next lesson, you will learn about two other ways of locating the data you want: sorting and filtering.

SORTING AND FILTERING DATA

In this lesson, you'll learn how to find data by sorting and filtering.

Access has many ways of finding and organizing data, and each is good for a certain situation. As you learned in Lesson 17, Find and Replace are great features when you're working with individual instances of a particular value, for example, finding Mr. Smith's record quickly. This lesson explains two other ways of finding what you need.

SORTING DATA

Even though you enter your records into the database in some sort of logical order, at some point, you'll want them in a different order. For instance, if we entered the dogs in our kennel according to registration number, we might later want to look at the list according to the dogs' birthdates, from oldest to youngest.

The Sort command is the perfect solution to this problem. With Sort, you can rearrange the records according to any field you like. You can sort in either ascending (A to Z, 1 to 10) or descending (Z to A, 10 to 1) order.

Which View? You can sort in either Form or Datasheet view, but I prefer Datasheet view because it shows many records at once.

Follow these steps to sort records:

1. Click anywhere in the field on which you want to sort.

2. Click the Sort Ascending button or Sort Descending button on the toolbar. Or if you prefer, select Records, Sort, and then choose Ascending or Descending from the submenu. Figure 18.1 shows our table of dogs sorted in Ascending order by birthdate.

Access sorted the table by this column.

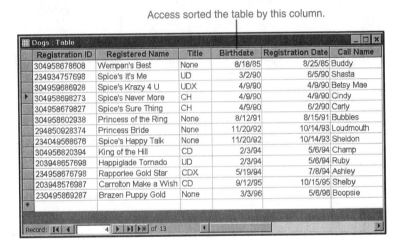

FIGURE 18.1   Access sorted this table in Ascending order by the Birthdate column.

3. If you want to restore the records to their presorted order, select Records, Remove Filter/Sort.

What Is Presorted Order?   If you defined a Primary Key field when you created your database (see Lesson 7), the records appear sorted in ascending order according to that field by default. This is the order they revert to when you remove a sort (as in step 3). If you save the datasheet or form without removing the sort, the sort order becomes part of that object.

FILTERING DATA

Filtering is for those times when you want to get many of the records out of the way so you can see the few that you're interested in. Filtering temporarily narrows down the number of records that appear, according to criteria you select.

Filters versus Queries   Queries also narrow down the records displayed, as you'll learn in Lesson 19. A filter is easier and quicker to use than a query, but a filter can't be saved as a separate object for later use. (However, you can save a filter as a query, as you'll learn later in this lesson.)

There are three ways to apply a filter: Filter by Selection, Filter by Form, and Advanced Filter/Sort. The first two are the most common for casual users, so we will cover them in the following sections. The third method is for advanced users only.

Sorting and Filtering   Neither of the filtering methods you'll learn in this lesson allow you to sort at the same time that you filter. However, it's easy enough to sort the filtered records, using the same sorting process you learned earlier in this lesson.

FILTER BY SELECTION

Filtering by selection is the easiest method of filtering, but before you can use it, you have to locate an instance of the value you want the filtered records to contain. For example, if you want to find all the dogs in your table that have earned the title of CD (Companion Dog), you must first locate a record that meets that criteria. You'll base the rest of the filter on that record.

To filter by selection, follow these steps:

1. In a field, find one instance of the value you want all filtered records to contain.

2. Select the value, as follows:

    • To find all records where the field value is identical to the selected value, select the entire field entry.

    • To find all records where the field begins with the selected value, select part of the field entry beginning with the first character.

    • To find all records where the field contains the selected value at any point, select part of the field entry beginning after the first character.

 3. Click the Filter by Selection button on the toolbar, or select Records, Filter, Filter by Selection. The records that match the criteria you selected appear.

Figure 18.2 shows the Dogs table filtered to show only dogs that have earned the CD title.

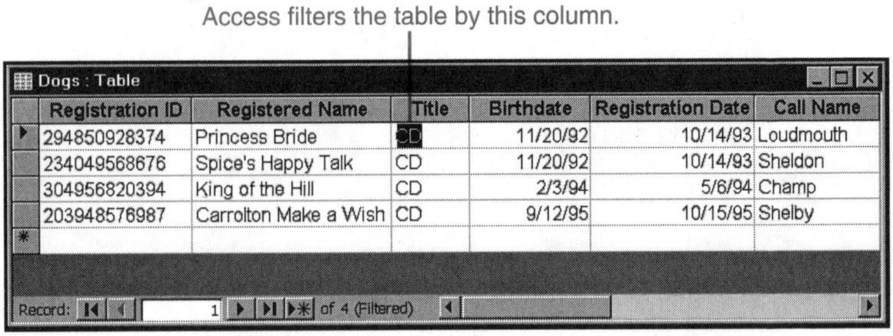

Access filters the table by this column.

Registration ID	Registered Name	Title	Birthdate	Registration Date	Call Name
294850928374	Princess Bride	CD	11/20/92	10/14/93	Loudmouth
234049568676	Spice's Happy Talk	CD	11/20/92	10/14/93	Sheldon
304956820394	King of the Hill	CD	2/3/94	5/6/94	Champ
203948576987	Carrolton Make a Wish	CD	9/12/95	10/15/95	Shelby

Dogs : Table

Record: 1 of 4 (Filtered)

FIGURE 18.2 The result of a filter; only the records that match the criteria appear.

Filtering by More Than One Criteria   With Filter by
Selection, you can filter by only one criteria at a time.
However, you can apply successive filters after the first
one to further narrow the list of matching records.

You can also filter for records that don't contain the selected
value. After selecting the value, right-click on it; then select Filter
Excluding Selection.

You can cancel a filter by clicking the Remove Filter button (the
same as the Apply Filter button), or by selecting Records, Remove
Filter/Sort.

FILTER BY FORM

Filtering by form is a more powerful filtering method than filtering by selection. With Filter by Form, you can filter by more than
one criteria at a time. You can also set up "or" filters, which find
records in which any one of several criteria is matched. You can
even enter logical expressions (such as "greater than a certain
value").

To filter by form, follow these steps:

1. In Datasheet or Form view, click the Filter by Form button
   on the toolbar or select Records, Filter, Filter by Form. A
   blank form appears, resembling an empty datasheet with
   a single record line.

2. Click in the field you want to set a criterion for, and a
   down-arrow appears for a drop-down list. Click on the
   arrow, and select the value you want from the list. Or you
   can type the value directly into the field if you prefer.

3. Enter as many criteria as you like in various fields. Figure
   18.3 shows two criteria, including a criteria that uses a
   less-than sign, a mathematical operator (explained in
   Lesson 19).

4. If you want to set up an "or" condition, click the Or tab at the bottom of the Filter by Form window, and enter the alternate criteria into that form. Notice that another Or tab appears when you fill this one, so you can add multiple "or" conditions.

5. After you enter your criteria, click the Apply Filter button on the toolbar. Your filtered data appears.

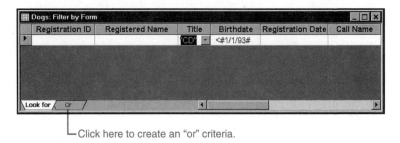

Click here to create an "or" criteria.

FIGURE **18.3**   This query finds all dogs that were born before 1/1/93 and have a CD (Companion Dog) title.

As with Filter by Selection, you can undo a filter by clicking the Filter button again or by selecting Records, Remove Filter/Sort.

SAVING YOUR FILTERED DATA AS A QUERY

Filters are a convenient alternative to creating a simple query from scratch. You can save a filter as a query, and use it as you would use a query; it even appears on your Queries list in the Database window. (You'll learn more about working with queries in Lesson 19.)

To save a filter as a query, follow these steps:

1. Display the filter in Query by Form view.

2. Select File, Save As Query or click the Save button on the toolbar. Access asks for a name for the new query.

3. Type a name and click OK. Access saves the filter.

In this lesson, you learned how to sort and filter your database. In the next lesson, you will begin learning about queries, a more sophisticated way of isolating and organizing information.

CREATING A
QUERY

In this lesson, you'll learn how a query can help you find the information you need, and how to create a simple one using the Simple Query Wizard. You'll also learn how to save and print query results.

WHAT IS A QUERY?

As you learned in Lesson 18, Access offers many ways to help you narrow down the information you're looking at, including sorting and filtering. A query is simply a more formal way to sort and filter.

Queries enable you to specify:

- Which fields you want to see.

- In what order the fields should appear.

- Filter criteria for each field (see Lesson 18).

- The order in which you want each field sorted (see Lesson 18).

TIP **Saving a Filter** When the primary purpose of the query is to filter, you may find it easier to create a filter and save it as a query. See Lesson 18 for details.

In this lesson, you'll create a simple query. In the next lesson (Lesson 20), you'll learn how to modify it to make it more powerful.

CREATING A SIMPLE QUERY USING QUERY WIZARD

The easiest way to create a query is with a Query Wizard, and the easiest Query Wizard is the Simple Query Wizard. (The other Query Wizards are "special-use" ones that you'll probably never need; they're described later in this lesson.)

The Simple Query Wizard lets you select the fields you want to display. You don't get to set criteria for including individual records, or specify a sort order. (You'll learn to do those things in Lesson 20.) This kind of simple query is useful when you want to weed out extraneous fields, but you still want to see every record.

 Select Query The query that the Simple Query Wizard creates is a basic version of a Select query. The Select query is the most common query type. You can select records, sort them, filter them, and perform simple calculations on the results (such as counting and averaging).

To create a simple Select query with the Simple Query Wizard, follow these steps:

1. Open the database you want to work with, and click on the Queries tab.

2. Click the New button. The New Query dialog box appears.

3. Click Simple Query Wizard; then click OK. The first box of the Simple Query Wizard appears, as shown in Figure 19.1. This screen may look familiar; it's similar to the first screen of the Form Wizard, described in Lesson 13.

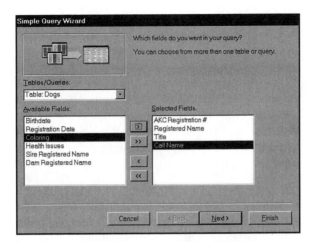

FIGURE 19.1   The Simple Query Wizard first asks what fields you want to include.

4. Choose the table from which you want to select fields from the Tables/Queries drop-down list. For example, I'm going to use Dogs.

5. Click on a field name in the Available Fields list; then click the > button to move it to the Selected Fields list. Repeat to move all the fields you want, or move them all at once with the >> button.

6. Select another table or query from the Tables/Queries list and add some of its fields to the Selected Fields list if you like. When you finish adding fields, click Next.

7. Next you're asked whether you want a Detail or a Summary query. Choose whichever you want—if you're not sure, stick with **Detail**, the default. If you choose **Summary**, the Summary Options button becomes available, which you can click on to open a dialog box of summary options. When you're finished, click Next. The next dialog box appears (see Figure 19.2).

Relationships Required If you are going to use two or more tables in your query, they must be joined with a relationship. See Lesson 25 to learn how to create relationships between tables.

8. Enter a title for the query in the What title do you want for your query? text box. I'm going to call mine Dog Names.

9. Click Finish to view the query results. Figure 19.3 shows my results.

This simple query is too simple; it has limited usefulness and doesn't show off any of Access's powerful query features. You could get the same results by hiding certain columns in datasheet view! Luckily, the Select query is much more powerful than the Simple Query Wizard makes it appear, as you'll see in the next lesson. But before you go there, take a look at a few basics that apply to any query.

FIGURE 19.2 Next, enter a title for your query.

Registration ID	Registered Name	Title	Call Name
203948576987	Carrolton Make a Wish	CD	Shelby
203948657698	Happiglade Tornado	UD	Ruby
230495869287	Brazen Puppy Gold	None	Boopsie
234049568676	Spice's Happy Talk	CD	Sheldon
234934757698	Spice's It's Me	UD	Shasta
234958876798	Rapporlee Gold Star	CDX	Ashley
294850928374	Princess Bride	CD	Loudmouth
304956820394	King of the Hill	CD	Champ
304958602938	Princess of the Ring	None	Bubbles
304958678608	Wempen's Best	None	Buddy
304958679827	Spice's Sure Thing	CH	Carly
304958698273	Spice's Never More	CH	Cindy
304959686928	Spice's Krazy 4 U	UDX	Betsy Mae

Record: ⏮ ◀ 1 ▶ ⏭ ▶* of 13

FIGURE 19.3 Here are the results of my simple query.

SAVING A QUERY

When you create a query, Access saves it automatically. You don't need to do anything special to save it. Just close the query window, and look on the Queries tab of the Database window. You'll see the query on the list.

TIP **Close the Query?** Close a query window the same way you close any window, by clicking its Close button (the X in the top-right corner).

RERUNNING A QUERY

At any time, you can rerun your query. If the data has changed since the last time you ran the query, the changes will be represented.

To rerun a query, follow these steps:

1. Open the database containing the query.

2. Click the Queries tab in the Database window.

3. Double-click the query you want to rerun, or click it once and then click the Open button (see Figure 19.4).

Double-click here to open the Dog Names query.

FIGURE 19.4   Redisplay any query by opening it from the Queries tab.

WORKING WITH QUERY RESULTS

Query results appear in Datasheet view, as shown in Figure 19.3. You can do anything to the records that you can do in a normal Datasheet view (see Lesson 11), including copying and deleting records, and changing field entries.

For example, let's say you wanted to update a sales database to change the Last Contacted field (a date) to today for every record. From your query results window, you could make that change. Or perhaps you want to delete all records for customers who haven't made a purchase in the last two years. You could delete the records from the query results window, and they would disappear from the table too.

Of course, with the latter example, it would be easier if the records were sorted according to the field in question, and the Simple Query Wizard you learned about in this lesson won't let you sort. However, in Lesson 20, you will learn about some other, more powerful Query Wizards that let you choose more options.

PRINTING QUERY RESULTS

The query results window not only edits like a datasheet but also prints like one. To print the query results, do the following:

1. Make sure the query results window is active.

2. Select File, Print, or press Ctrl+P. The Print dialog box appears.

3. Select any print options you want (refer to Lesson 10); then click OK.

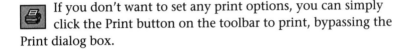 If you don't want to set any print options, you can simply click the Print button on the toolbar to print, bypassing the Print dialog box.

OTHER QUERY WIZARDS

Access's query features are powerful; they can do amazingly complicated calculations and comparisons on many tables at once. You can create queries with their own dialog boxes for custom entry of special criteria, link a query to external databases (databases in other programs), and much more.

Unfortunately, the process for creating a lot of these powerful queries is quite complicated. It's enough to give casual users a headache. That's why in this book, we stick to the basic Select type of query, which does almost everything an average user needs to do.

There are some intermediate Access Query Wizards that will help you experiment with more complex query types without causing too much stress. Each of these Query Wizards appears on the list when you click the New button from the Queries tab. We won't cover any of them in this book, but you may want to try them out yourself:

- **Crosstab Query Wizard** Displays summarized values, such as sums, counts, and averages, from one field, and groups them by one set of facts listed down the left side of the datasheet as row headings and another set of facts listed across the top of the datasheet as column headings.

- **Find Unmatched Query Wizard** Compares two tables and finds all records that do not appear in both tables (based on comparing certain fields).

- **Find Duplicates Query Wizard** The opposite of Find Unmatched. It compares two tables and finds all records that appear in both.

In this lesson, you learned to create a simple query, and to save, edit, and print query results. In the next lesson, you will learn how to modify the query you created.

MODIFYING A QUERY

LESSON 20

20

In this lesson, you'll learn how to modify the query you created in Lesson 19 using Query Design view.

INTRODUCING QUERY DESIGN VIEW

In Lesson 19, you created a simple query using the Simple Query Wizard, which selected and displayed fields from a table. There's a lot more you can do with your query when you enter Query Design view.

Query Design view is much like Table Design view and Form Design view, both of which you've encountered earlier in this book. In Query Design view, you can change the rules that govern your query results.

OPENING A QUERY IN QUERY DESIGN VIEW

To open an existing query in Query Design view, follow these steps:

1. Open the database that contains the query you want to edit.

2. Click the Queries tab.

3. Click the query you want to edit; then click the Design button.

The query created in Lesson 19 is shown in Query Design view in Figure 20.1. You'll learn how to edit it in this lesson.

The tables used in the query are shown here. This query has
only one. Each table has its own box listing its fields.

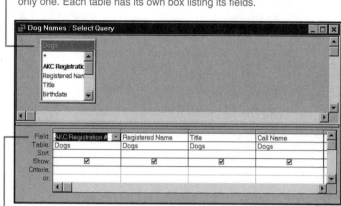

Each field used in the query has its own column.

FIGURE 20.1 In Query Design view, you can edit a query you
have created.

STARTING A NEW QUERY IN QUERY DESIGN VIEW

Instead of using the Simple Query Wizard to begin your query, as
you did in Lesson 19, you can begin a query from scratch in
Query Design view. As you become more familiar with Access
queries, you may find that this is faster and easier than using a
wizard.

To begin a new query in Query Design view, follow these steps:

1. Open the database in which you want the query.

2. Click the Queries tab in the Database window.

3. Click the New button.

4. Click Design View and click OK. The Show Table dialog
   box appears, listing all the tables in the database.

5. Click on a table you want to work with; then click the
   Add button. Repeat for each table you want to add. Don't

forget, there must be a relationship already established between the tables you use if you use more than one (see Lesson 25).

6. Click Close when you finish adding tables. The Query Design view window opens, as in Figure 20.1, except there won't be any fields selected yet.

ADDING FIELDS TO A QUERY

If you created your query from scratch (as in the preceding set of steps), the first thing you need to do is add the fields you want to work with. You can also use this same procedure to add fields to an existing query.

Adding More Tables   You can add tables to your query at any time. Just click the Show Table button on the toolbar or select Query, Show Table. Then select the table(s) you want and click Add. Click Close to return to your query design.

There are three ways to add a field to a query. All methods are easy; try all of them to see which you prefer. Here's the first method:

1. Click in the Table row of the first blank column. A down-arrow button appears, indicating that a drop-down list is available.

2. Open the drop-down list and select a table. The tables available on the list are the same as the table windows that appear at the top of the query design window.

3. Click in the Field row directly above the table name you just selected. A down-arrow button appears, indicating that a drop-down list is available.

4. Open the drop-down list and select a field. The fields listed come from the tables you selected for the query.

The field's name appears in the Field row, in the column where you selected it.

 Only One Table?   If you are using only one table in the query, you can skip the first two steps in this procedure.

Here's the second method of adding a field:

1. Scroll through the list of fields in the desired table window at the top of the Query Design box, until you find the field you want to add.

2. Click on the field name and drag it into the Field row of the first empty column. The field's name appears where you dragged it.

The third method is to simply double-click the field name in the field list. It moves to the first available slot in the query grid.

DELETING A FIELD

There are two ways to delete a field from your query:

- Click anywhere in the column and select Edit, Delete Column.

 - Position the mouse pointer directly above the column, so the pointer turns into a down-pointing black arrow. Then click to select the entire column and press the Delete key; or click the Cut button on the toolbar.

 Cut versus Delete   If you cut the column instead of deleting it, you can paste it back into the query. Just select the column where you want it, and then click the Paste button or choose Edit, Paste. Be careful, though; the pasted column replaces the selected one. The selected column doesn't move over to make room for it. Select an empty column if you don't want to replace an existing one.

ADDING CRITERIA

Criteria will be familiar to you if you read Lesson 18, which deals with filters. Criteria enables you to choose which records will appear in your query results. For example, I could limit my list of dogs to those whose birth dates were before 8/5/94.

> **TIP**   **Filters versus Queries**   If the primary reason for creating the query is to filter, you may want to create the filter part first using one of the procedures described in Lesson 18, and then you can save the filter as a query. You can open that query in Query Design view and fine-tune it as needed.

To set criteria for a field that you've added to your query, follow these steps:

1. In Query Design view, click the Criteria row in the desired field's column.

2. Type the criteria you want to use, as shown in Figure 20.2. Table 20.1 provides some examples you could have entered in Figure 20.2 and the subsequent results.

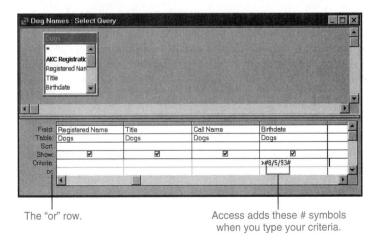

The "or" row.   Access adds these # symbols
                       when you type your criteria.

FIGURE 20.2   Enter criteria into the Criteria row in the appropriate field's column.

In Figure 20.2, Access added # symbols because we are working with a date. For other types of criteria, Access adds other symbols, like quotation marks around a text or number string.

TABLE 20.1   SAMPLE CRITERIA FOR QUERIES

ENTER THIS	TO GET RECORDS WHERE THIS VALUE IS
8/5/93	Exactly 8/5/93
<8/5/93	Before 8/5/93
>8/5/93	After 8/5/93
>=8/5/93	8/5/93 or after
<=8/5/93	8/5/93 or before
Not <8/5/93	Not before 8/5/93
Not >8/5/93	Not after 8/5/93

Text, Too   You can also enter text as a criteria. The < and > (before and after) operators apply to alphabetical order with text. For instance, **<C** finds text that begins with A or B.

Did you notice the "or" row under the Criteria row in Figure 20.2? You can enter more criteria using that line. The query will find records where any of the criteria is true. When you enter criteria into the "or" row, another "or" row appears, so you can enter more.

What About "And"?   When you have two criteria that must both be true, you can put them together in a single Criteria row, with the word "And." For instance, you might want birth dates that were between 12/1/93 and 12/1/95. It would all be in a single Criteria row, like this: >12/1/93 And <12/1/95.

SORTING A FIELD IN A QUERY

After all this complicated criteria discussion, you will be happy to know that sorting is fairly straightforward. To sort any field, just follow these steps from the query results window:

1. Click in the sort row for the field you want to sort. A down arrow for a drop-down list appears.

2. Open the drop-down list and select Ascending or Descending.

Later, if you want to cancel sorting for this field, repeat these steps, but select (not sorted). Refer back to Lesson 18 for more information about sorting.

SHOWING OR HIDING A FIELD

Some fields are included in your query only so you can filter or sort based on them. You may not necessarily be interested in seeing that field in the query results. For instance, you may want to limit your query to all dogs born before 8/5/93, but you don't want each dog's birth date to appear in the query.

To exclude a field from appearing in the query results, deselect the check box in the Show row. To include it again, select the check box again.

VIEWING QUERY RESULTS

When you're ready to see the results of your query, click the Run button on the Query Design toolbar or select Query, Run. Your results appear in a window that resembles a datasheet (see Figure 20.3).

FIGURE 20.3   The results of a kennel query based on birthdates.

In this lesson, you learned to modify and strengthen your queries. In the next lesson, you will learn how to create a simple, attractive report suitable for printing and distribution to others.

CREATING A SIMPLE REPORT

In this lesson, you'll learn how to create reports in Access using AutoReport and Report Wizard.

WHY CREATE REPORTS?

You've learned many ways to organize and view your data, but until now each method has focused on on-screen use. Forms help with data entry on-screen, and queries help you find information and display the results on-screen.

You can print any table, form, or query, but the results will be less than professional looking because those tools are not designed to be printed. Reports, on the other hand, are designed specifically to be printed and shared with other people. With a report, you can generate professional results that you can be proud of, whether you're distributing them on paper or publishing them on the Internet.

There are several ways to create a report, ranging from easy-but-limited (AutoReport) to difficult-but-very-flexible (Report Design view). The intermediate choice is Report Wizard, which offers some flexibility along with a fairly easy procedure.

USING AUTOREPORT TO CREATE A REPORT

If you want a plain, no-frills report based on a single table or query, AutoReport is for you. You can go back and improve its appearance later, when you learn about customizing reports in Lesson 22.

You can create either a tabular or a columnar report. A tabular report resembles a datasheet, and a columnar report resembles a form. They are equally easy to create.

To create a report with AutoReport, follow these steps:

1. Open the database containing the table or query on which you want to report.

2. Click the Reports tab in the Database window, and click the New button. The New Report dialog box appears (see Figure 21.1).

3. Click on AutoReport: Columnar or AutoReport: Tabular.

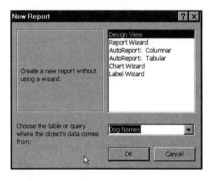

Figure 21.1   Choose one of the AutoReports from this window.

4. In the drop-down list at the bottom of the dialog box, select the table or query on which you want to base the report.

 Multiple Tables?   AutoReports can use only one table or query. If you want to create an AutoReport that uses several tables, first create a query based on those tables, and then base the AutoReport on the query.

5. Click OK. The report appears in Print Preview. See the "Viewing and Printing Reports in Print Preview" section later in this lesson to learn what to do next.

The AutoReports' output is not much better than a raw printout from a table or form, as you can see in Print Preview. If you want a better looking report, try Report Wizard.

CREATING A REPORT WITH REPORT WIZARD

The Report Wizard offers a good compromise between ease-of-use and flexibility. With Report Wizard, you can use multiple tables and queries and choose a layout and format for your report.

Follow these steps to create a report with Report Wizard:

1. Open the database containing the table or query on which you want to report.

2. Click the Reports tab in the Database window, and click the New button. The New Report dialog box appears (see Figure 21.1).

3. Click Report Wizard, and click OK. The Report Wizard starts (see Figure 21.2).

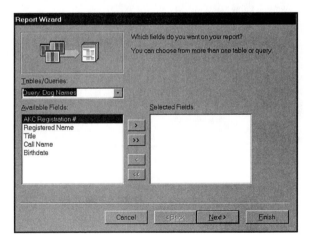

FIGURE 21.2   The first Report Wizard screen.

> **Multiple Tables/Queries Allowed**   You don't need to
> select a table or query from the drop-down list in the New
> Report dialog box in step 3, because you'll be selecting
> tables and queries in step 4 instead, as part of the wizard.

4. Open the Tables/Queries drop-down list, and select a
   table or query from which you want to include fields.

5. Click a field in the Available Fields list, and then click the
   > button to move it to the Selected Fields list. Repeat this
   step to select all the fields you want, or click >> to move
   all the fields over at once.

6. If desired, select another table or query from the Tables/
   Queries list and repeat step 5. When you finish selecting
   fields, click Next. The next screen of the wizard appears
   (see Figure 21.3).

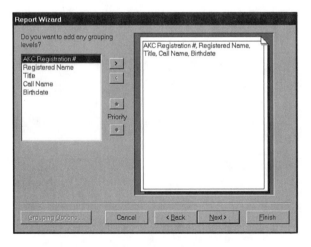

FIGURE 21.3   Set your report's grouping.

7. If you want the records grouped by any of the fields you
   selected, click on the field, and click the > button. You
   can select several grouping levels in the order you want
   them. Then click Next to move on.

Grouping? By default, there are no groups. You have to select a field and click the > button to create a grouping. Grouping sets off each group on the report. If you use a field to group, the Grouping Options button becomes active, and you can click on it to specify precise grouping settings.

8. Next you're asked what sort order you want to use (see Figure 21.4). If you want sorted records, open the top drop-down list and select a field to sort by. Select up to four sorts from the drop-down lists; then click Next.

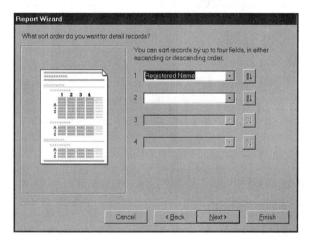

FIGURE 21.4 Set the sort order.

Ascending or Descending? By default, the sort is in ascending order (A–Z). Click the AZ button next to the box to change the sort order to descending (Z–A) if you like.

9. In the next dialog box (see Figure 21.5), choose a layout option from the Layout area. When you click on an option button, the sample in the box changes to show you what you selected.

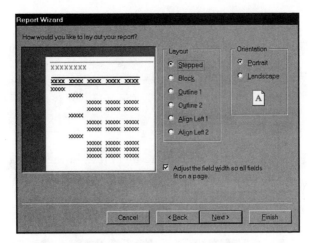

FIGURE 21.5   Choose the layout of your report.

> **Where Are All the Layouts?**   If you didn't choose any groupings in your report, your layout choices will be limited to three: Columnar, Tabular, and Justified. The layouts shown in Figure 21.5 are unique to grouped reports.

10. Choose which orientation your printed report will have: Portrait (across the narrow edge of the paper) or Landscape (across the wide edge of the paper). Then click Next to continue.

11. In the next wizard dialog box, you're asked to choose a report style. Several are listed; click one to see a sample of it; then click Next when you're satisfied with your choice.

12. Finally, you're asked for a report title. Enter one in the Report text box, and click Finish to see your report in Print Preview (see Figure 21.6).

Click here to print   Zoom in   Leave Print   See the report in 1,
immediately.   or out.   Preview.   2, or 4-page views.

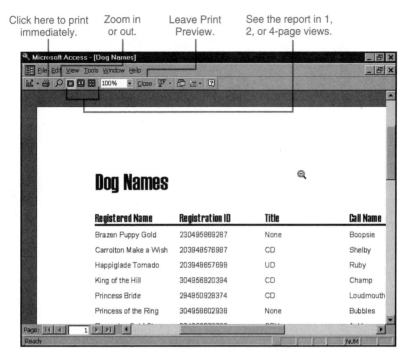

FIGURE 21.6 Here's a simple report with no grouping.

VIEWING AND PRINTING REPORTS IN PRINT PREVIEW

When you finish a report with either Report Wizard or
AutoReport, the report appears in Print Preview (as shown in Figure 21.6). From here, you can print the report, if you're happy
with it, or you can go to Report Design view to make changes.
(You'll learn more about this in Lesson 22.)

If you want to print the report and specify any print options (such
as number of copies), open the File menu and select Print. If you
want a quick hard copy, click the Print button on the toolbar. To
go to Report Design view, click Close. (Report Design view is actually open; it's just obscured by the Print Preview window.)

In this lesson, you learned to create and print a simple report. In
the next lesson, you will learn how to work in Report Design view
to customize your report.

22

CUSTOMIZING A REPORT

In this lesson, you'll learn to use Report Design view to make your report more attractive.

ENTERING REPORT DESIGN VIEW

When you finish previewing a report you've created, just close Print Preview and you're automatically in Report Design view.

If you want to come back to Report Design view later, from the Database window, perform these steps:

1. Click the Reports tab.

2. Click the report you want to modify.

3. Click the Design button. The report appears in Design view, as shown in Figure 22.1.

Report Design view may seem familiar to you; it looks a lot like Form Design view. Almost everything you learned about editing forms in Lessons 14 and 16 applies also to reports. Just like Form Design view, there is a toolbox of common editing tools, and you can add all the special elements that you learned about in Lesson 15.

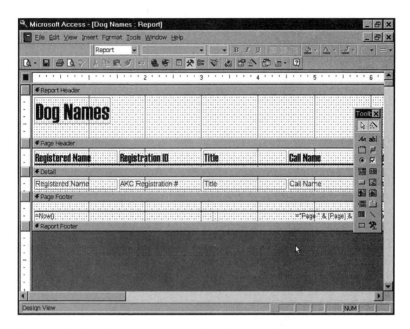

FIGURE 22.1   The report created in the previous lesson, in Design view.

WORKING WITH OBJECTS ON YOUR REPORT

Working with report objects in Report Design view is exactly the same as working with objects in Form Design view. An object is any control, such as a field name or a title. Turn back to Lesson 14 for the full story, or follow the brief review here:

Selecting objects   Just like in Form Design view, you select an object on your report by clicking it. Selection handles (little squares in the corners) appear around it. See Lesson 14 for more details.

Moving objects   To move an object, first select it. Then position the mouse pointer over a border so the pointer turns into an open black hand. Then click and drag the object to a new location.

Resizing objects   First, select the object. Then position the mouse pointer over one of the selection handles and drag the handle to resize the object.

Formatting text objects   Use the Font and Font Size drop-down lists on the toolbar to choose fonts; then use the Bold, Italic, and Underline toolbar buttons to set special attributes.

You can also add graphic lines and objects to reports, just like you do with forms. Refer back to Lesson 16, "Adding Graphics to Forms."

 Access on the Web   You can assign hyperlinks to objects on your forms and reports, as you'll learn in Lesson 27. They aren't "hot" (that is, they don't actually link) on the printouts, but if you save a report in Microsoft Word format, the hyperlinks can be activated when you open the document in Word.

ADDING AND REMOVING FIELDS

You can add more fields to your report at any time. Follow these steps to do so:

 1. If you don't see the Field List, select View, Field List or click the Field List button on the toolbar. A floating box appears listing all the fields in the table you are using.

2. Drag any field from the Field List into the report. Place it anywhere in the Detail area that you want.

Don't worry if the field isn't in the right place or if it overlaps another field; you'll learn to fix that in the following section. To delete a field, select it by clicking it, then press the Delete key. This deletes the reference to the field from the report, but it remains in the table from which it came.

Arranging Your New Fields

When you add a field to your report, you're actually adding two things: a label and a text box. These two elements are bound together: The label describes the text box, and the text box represents the actual field that will be used (see Figure 22.2). You can change the label without affecting the text box; for instance, you could change the label on the Coloring field to Dog Color without affecting the contents. To change a label, just click it and then retype.

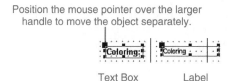

Position the mouse pointer over the larger
handle to move the object separately.

Text Box   Label

Figure 22.2   The text box and its label.

🖐 By default, when you move the text box, the label follows. When you position the mouse pointer over the border of the text box, and the pointer changes to an open hand, that's your signal that the label will follow the text box when you drag it.

🖐 However, you can also move the text box and the label separately. Notice that in the upper-left corner of each, there is a selection handle (square) that's bigger than the others. When you position the mouse pointer over that handle, the cursor becomes a pointing hand. That's your signal that you can click-and-drag the object separately from the other.

Moving the label separately can come in handy when you don't want the label to appear in its default position (to the left of the text box). For instance, you may want the label to appear above the text box.

ADDING LABELS

 In the preceding section, you saw how to add a field: A text box plus a label, both bound together. But you can also add labels by themselves, with extra text in them that is not necessarily associated with a particular field—for instance, an informational note about the report in general. Just click on the Label button in the toolbox. Then click anywhere on the report and start typing. When you finish, click anywhere outside the label.

ADDING A CALCULATED TEXT BOX

The most common thing that text boxes hold is references to fields, as you have seen in this lesson. However, text boxes have another purpose; they can also hold calculations based on values in different fields.

Creating a calculated text box is a bit complicated; first you have to create an unbound text box (that is, one that's not associated with any particular field). Then you have to enter the calculation into the text box. Follow these steps:

1. Click the Text Box tool in the toolbox, and click-and-drag on the report to create a text box.

2. Change the label to reflect what's going to go into that box. For instance, if it's going to be Sales Tax, change it to that. Position the label where you want it.

3. Click in the text box and type the formula you want calculated. (See the following section for guidance.)

4. Click anywhere outside the text box when you finish.

RULES FOR CREATING CALCULATIONS

The formulas you enter into your calculated text box use standard mathematical controls:

+   Add
–   Subtract
*   Multiply
/   Divide

All formulas begin with an equals sign (=), and all field names are in parentheses. Here are some examples:

> To calculate a total price by multiplying the value in the Quantity field by the value in the Price field, enter **=(Quantity)*(Price)**.
>
> To calculate a 25% discount off the value in the Cost field, enter **=(Cost)*.075**.
>
> To add the total of the values in three fields, enter **(Field1)+(Field2)+(Field3)**.

 TIP   **More Room**   If you run out of room in the text box when typing your formula press Shift+F2 to open a Zoom box, where there's more room.

In this lesson, you learned to customize your report by adding and removing objects, moving them around, and creating calculations. In the next lesson, you'll learn how to create a chart based on a table or query in your database.

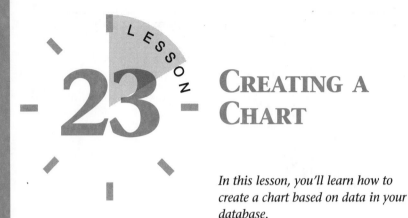

CREATING A CHART

In this lesson, you'll learn how to create a chart based on data in your database.

THE CHART ADVANTAGE

Have you ever noticed how people's eyes glaze over when you present them with a stack of statistics? Your message will come across more clearly if you present your information in a format that's easy to understand, like a chart. One glance at a chart can communicate the message contained in a hundred pages of raw data.

For instance, let's say I want to know which colors of dogs my kennel owns the most of. I could print a report that lists all the dogs and their colorings, manually count how many of each color there are, and divide each color total by the total number of dogs. This technique would give me the percentage of each color. Creating a chart that shows the percentage of each coloring would be much easier.

Charts are also good for tracking information over time. For instance, in a sales organization, you could chart the sales volume for each sales person by month, or you could chart how many units of each product you sell per month (or week, or year).

CREATING A CHART

Access considers a chart to be a type of report, so you create one much like you create a report. Just follow along with the Wizard.

The Chart Wizard works basically the same for all charts, but the screens vary a little. So first, we'll create a simple pie chart based on a single field, then we'll try a bar chart.

CREATING A SIMPLE PIE CHART

A pie chart is good for relating parts to a whole.

To create a pie chart, follow these steps:

1. Open the database that contains the table or query that you want to chart.

2. Click the Reports tab in the database window, then click the New button. The New Report dialog box appears.

3. Select Chart Wizard.

4. Open the drop-down list at the bottom of the dialog box and select the table or query that contains the data you want to chart. Then click OK, and the Chart Wizard starts (see Figure 23.1).

Click here to move a field to the Fields for Chart list.

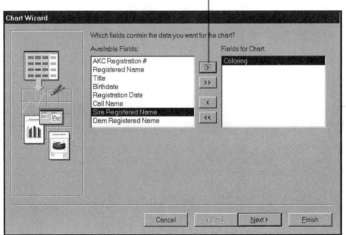

FIGURE 23.1   The Chart Wizard first asks which fields you want to include.

 Don't Select Too Many!   Select only one field for a pie chart or two fields for most other chart types. Otherwise, either all the fields will not show up on the chart or the chart will look crowded.

5. Select a field from the Available Fields list, and click the >
button to move it to the Fields for Chart list. Since I'm
making a pie chart, which can accommodate only one
field, I'll just select Coloring. Click Next > to move on.

6. Choose which chart type you want (see Figure 23.2). Click
on one of the pie chart pictures and read the description
that appears. Notice that most chart types have both
three-dimensional and two-dimensional versions. When
you're satisfied with your choice, click Next >.

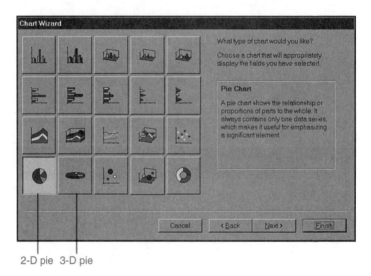

2-D pie 3-D pie

FIGURE 23.2   Select the chart type.

7. Next you'll see a layout screen. This screen is important
with more complicated charts, but with our pie chart,
there's nothing much to do, so just click Next > to move
on.

8. The last Chart Wizard screen asks for a title. Enter one.

9. Click Yes, display a legend or No, don't display a legend.
(I recommend Yes if you don't know which to pick.) Then
click Finish. Your chart appears in Print Preview. Mine is
shown in Figure 23.3.

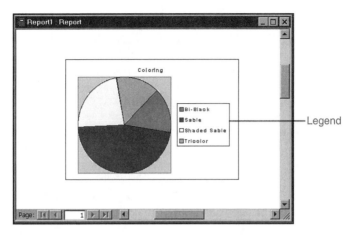

FIGURE 23.3   The finished pie chart.

Line and bar charts both show data over time. For instance, you might show your sales over several years. Let's do that in the following steps:

1. Follow the first three steps of the procedure in "Creating a Simple Pie Chart" earlier in this lesson, so that the New Report dialog box is displayed and you've chosen Chart Wizard as the report type.

2. Choose the table or query you want to work with from the drop-down list. For the Northwind Traders database example, I'm picking Sales by year. Then click OK, and the first screen of the Chart Wizard is displayed.

3. Add the fields you want to work with to the Fields for Chart list, as you did with the pie chart. You'll want to pick at least two fields, since a bar chart has two axes. For instance, I'm picking Subtotal and Year. Then click Next >.

4. You'll be asked to select a chart type (as in Figure 23.2). Click one of the bar charts then click Next >. You'll see the layout screen (see Figure 23.4).

New Database?   Since our kennel example doesn't have appropriate fields in it for this example, I'll be using the Northwind Traders database, the sample database that came with Access. It's in the Samples folder in your Access folder on your hard disk. You can open it and follow along if you like. See Lesson 6 for a refresher on opening database files.

5. If the fields are not correct, drag them from the chart back to the right side of the dialog box to remove them from the chart, then drag the correct fields onto the correct spots. When everything is correct, click Next >.

6. In the next box that appears, enter a title, choose whether to use a legend, then click Finish.

7. Depending on the table you used, you may be asked to enter extra information. For example, I was asked to input a start date and an end date. I used 1/1/93 as the start and 1/1/95 as the end date.

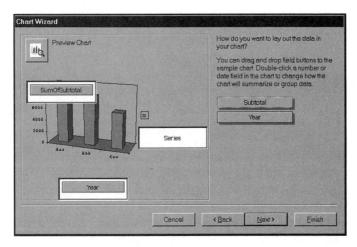

Figure 23.4   Make sure that Access has correctly guessed how you want the fields positioned on the chart.

After you've answered all the questions, your chart appears. Mine is shown in Figure 23.5.

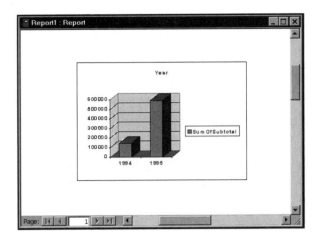

FIGURE 23.5   A simple bar chart created with the Northwind Traders database that comes with Access.

USING PRINT PREVIEW

Since the chart is considered a report, the procedure for working with it in Print Preview is exactly the same as the procedure you learned in Lesson 21. You can print by clicking the Print button or close the Print Preview box by clicking the Close button.

SAVING A CHART

To save a chart, just exit from Print Preview by clicking the Close button. You'll get a message asking if you want to save the changes to your report. Click Yes, and you'll be prompted for a name. Type the chart's name as you want it to appear on the Reports tab of the Database window, then click OK. Access dumps you into Design view, where you can modify your chart.

MODIFYING A CHART IN MICROSOFT GRAPH

To modify a chart, use a program called Microsoft Graph. It's a mini-program that all the Microsoft Office products (such as Word, Excel, Access, and PowerPoint) share.

To open your chart in Microsoft Graph for modifications, follow these steps:

1. Open the database that contains the chart and click the Reports tab of the Database window.

2. Click the chart you want to modify, then click the Design button. The report opens in Design view.

3. Double-click the chart. Microsoft Graph opens, with your chart displayed (see Figure 23.6).

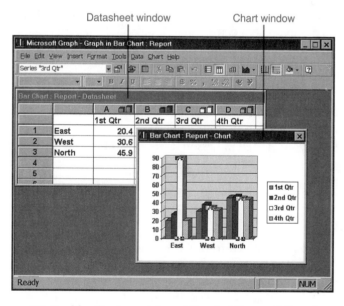

FIGURE 23.6   My chart open for editing in Microsoft Graph.

Notice that Microsoft Graph shows two windows: a Chart window, which displays a replica of your chart, and a Datasheet window, which displays the statistics that went into making the chart. You can edit in both windows.

Don't Alter Your Data! Microsoft Graph allows you to change your data in the Datasheet window, but don't do it if you are relying on the chart being accurate! If you change the data on the datasheet, it will no longer reflect what's in your database.

To edit the content of a cell in the datasheet, just click in the cell where you want to edit and type a new value. Even though you should not change the numerical values that make up the chart, you can safely change any label. For instance, I might change "Pure sable" to "Pure for sable," without compromising the integrity of my chart. That change would appear only in the chart legend, though, not in the table on which the chart was based.

To change the formatting of your chart, double-click any part of the chart, and a dialog box pops up enabling you to change its properties. Experiment by double-clicking every part of your chart. You can always click Cancel to close the dialog box.

When you are finished editing your chart, just close the Microsoft Graph window to return to Access. You'll be asked whether you want to save your changes; answer Yes.

In this lesson, you learned to create, print, save, and modify a chart. In the next lesson, you will learn how to create mailing labels.

CREATING MAILING LABELS

In this lesson, you'll learn how to make mailing labels using names and addresses in a database.

EASY MAILING LABELS WITH ACCESS

If you have ever done mass mailings to club members, customers, or even friends, the worst part was probably addressing all those envelopes. Access lets you create mailing labels directly from an address book database (or any other database).

To create mailing labels, use the Label Wizard. Mailing labels are a type of report, so you'll start the process from the Reports tab of your database.

Which Database? I'm going to use a sample database I created using Access's Contact Management template, using Access's own sample data. You can create this same database by following the steps for creating a new database in Lesson 5.

CREATING MAILING LABELS WITH THE LABEL WIZARD

To create mailing labels from a table that contains names and addresses, follow these steps:

1. Open the database you want to work with and click the Reports tab.

2. Click the New button. The New Report dialog box appears. In it, click Label Wizard.

3. Open the drop-down list at the bottom of the box and select the table or query from which to pull the names and addresses. Then click OK. The first screen of the Label Wizard appears (see Figure 24.1).

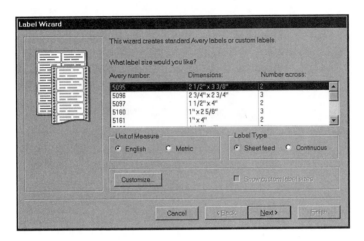

FIGURE 24.1   Label Wizard starts out by asking you what size labels you'll be using.

4. Choose the label type from the list. If there are only a few labels listed, make sure the Show Custom Label Sizes check box is deselected. (It must be deselected to see the standard label types.)

Don't Know the Avery Number?   If you don't know the Avery number for your label, move through the labels listed until you find one with dimensions that match those of your labels. You can also create a custom label.

5. Click Sheet feed or Continuous. Sheet-fed labels are single sheets; continuous labels are joined to the previous and next sheet at the top, and have perforated strips on the side that feed through a dot-matrix printer.

6. Click Next > when you've entered your label information.

7. Next choose a font from the Font name drop-down list, and a font size from the Font size drop-down list (see Figure 24.2).

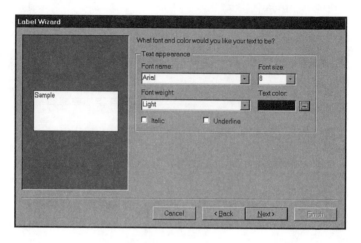

Figure 24.2   Choose settings for the text to be printed on the labels.

Don't make the Font Too Big!   If you need to print multiple lines on each label, make sure that the font size you select is small enough that all lines will fit. For mailing labels, 8 or 10 point type works well; it is large enough to be read by U.S. Postal Service machines, but small enough that you can fit several lines on each label.

8. With some fonts, you can choose a font weight. Open the Font weight drop-down list and choose a weight. **Normal** will work well in most cases.

9. If you would like color labels (and you have a color printer), choose a different color from the Text color list. To do so, click the button next to the Text color box and select from the Color dialog box that appears; click OK to return.

Avoid Light Colors!   If you're making labels to be sent through the U.S. Postal Service, keep in mind that their machines can't read light-colored ink like yellow.

10. Click the Italic or the Underline check box if you want the text formatted with those attributes. Then click Next > to continue.

11. Next, Access asks which fields to include on the label. Select a field from the Available Fields list and click the > button to move it to the Prototype label (see Figure 24.3).

12. Continue selecting fields until all fields you want to use appear on the label. Don't forget to add spaces between fields on the same line (for instance, a space between the first and last name). You can press Enter to start a new line on the label. Then click Next > to continue.

I typed a space here.

Label Wizard

What would you like on your mailing label?

Construct your label on the right by choosing fields from the left. You may also type text that you would like to see on every label right onto the prototype.

Available fields:

ContactID
FirstName
LastName
Dear
Address
City
StateOrProvince

Prototype label:

{FirstName} {LastName}
{Address}

Cancel   < Back   Next >   Finish

I pressed Enter here and here.

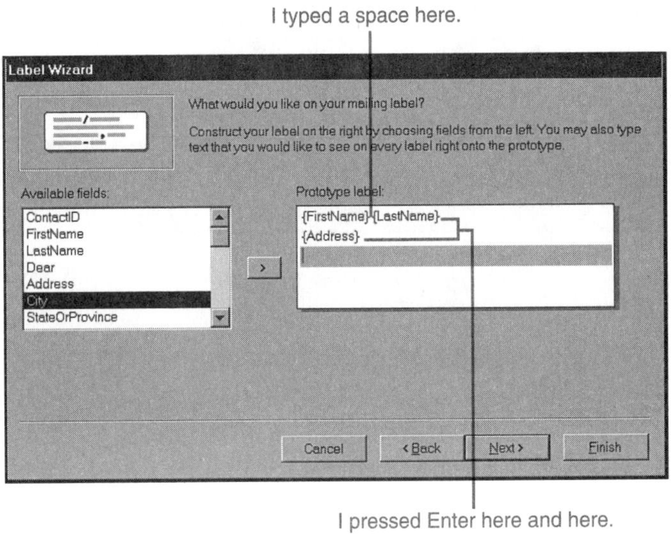

FIGURE 24.3   Adding fields to your label.

Adding Other Text   If there is text that you want to appear on every label, you can type it as you enter fields. One example is a comma to separate the City and State fields.

13. If you would like your labels sorted by a particular field, select it on the next screen that appears (see Figure 24.4) and click the > button to move it to the Sort by list. For instance, some bulk mailings require you to sort by ZIP code (or PostalCode). Click Next > to continue.

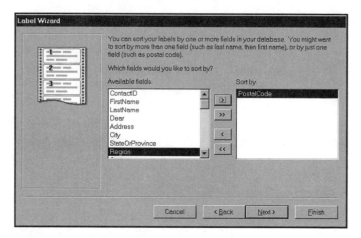

FIGURE 24.4   Select which field(s) you want to sort by, if any.

Order Is Important!   If you pick more than one field to sort by, Access sorts the records first by the first field you select, then by the second, and so on. So it's important to choose the field that you want to sort by first. If they're in the wrong order, click the << button to remove them all from the Sort by list; then start over.

14. In the last screen, you're asked for a title. Enter one and click Finish. Your labels appear in Print Preview, just like any other report. Mine are shown in Figure 24.5.

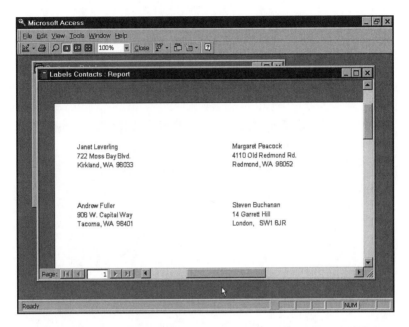

FIGURE 24.5   Mailing labels created by the Label Wizard, in Print Preview.

PRINTING LABELS

Since the labels, like a chart, are considered a report, the procedure for working with them in Print Preview is exactly the same as the procedure you learned in Lesson 21. You can print by clicking the Print button, or close the Print Preview box by clicking the Close button.

SAVING LABELS

To save your labels, just exit from Print Preview. You'll see the labels appear in the Database window on the Reports tab. Unlike with a chart or report, Report Design view does not appear automatically when you close Print Preview.

MODIFYING YOUR LABELS

If you want to modify the labels, you can enter Report Design view and make changes, just as you would with any report. Just click on the labels on the Reports tab, then click Design. Your label design appears, as shown in Figure 24.6.

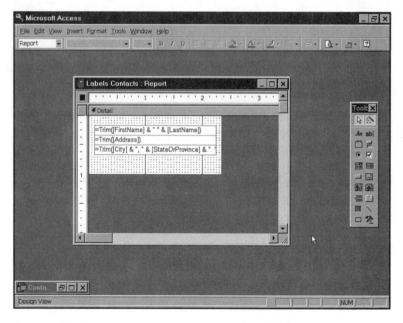

FIGURE 24.6   You can modify your label, just as you would modify any report.

Use all the same editing techniques that you learned in Lesson 22, "Customizing a Report," to make changes to your label.

In this lesson, you learned how to create mailing labels. In the next lesson, you will learn how to create relationships among tables.

CREATING RELATIONSHIPS BETWEEN TABLES

In this lesson, you'll learn how to link two or more tables together so you can work with them as you would a single table.

WHY CREATE RELATIONSHIPS?

Lesson 2 encouraged you to make separate tables for information that was not directly related. As you've learned along the way, when you create forms, queries, and reports, you can pull information from more than one table easily. But this works best when there is a well-defined relationship between the tables.

Let's say, for instance, that I had two tables containing information about my customers. One table, Customers, contained their names and addresses, and the other, Orders, contained their orders. The two tables would have a common field: Customer ID#. All records in the Orders table would correspond to a record in the Customers table. (This is called a "many-to-one" relationship because there could be many orders for one customer.)

As another example, in my kennel database, I have several tables describing my dogs and their activities. I have a table listing all the different colorings a dog can have. I could create a relationship between the Dogs table and the Coloring table, matching up each dog's coloring field with one of the accepted colors listed in the Coloring table. This would ensure that I didn't record any dog's coloring as a type that's not allowed.

More Complicated I'm showing you only simple examples in this lesson. For more information on relationships, see your Access documentation or *Using Microsoft Access 97, Special Edition*, published by Que.

CREATING A RELATIONSHIP BETWEEN TABLES

To create a relationship between tables, open the Relationships window and add relationships there. Follow these steps:

1. In the database select Tools, Relationships.

2. If you have not selected any tables yet, the Show Table dialog box (see Figure 25.1) appears automatically. If it doesn't, Open the Relationships menu and select Show Table or click the Show Table toolbar button.

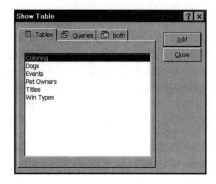

FIGURE 25.1   Add tables to your Relationships window using this dialog box.

3. Click a table that you want to use for a relationship, then click the Add button.

4. Repeat step 3 to select all the tables you want, then click Close. Each table appears in its own box on the Relationships window, as shown in Figure 25.2.

Make it Bigger   If you can't clearly see all the fields in a table's list, drag the border of its box to make it large enough to see everything. I've done that in Figure 25.2 to make the Dogs table completely visible.

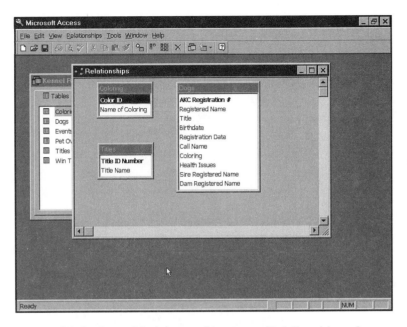

FIGURE 25.2   I've added three tables to my Relationships window, for this example.

5. Click a field in one table that you want to link to another table. For instance, I'm going to link the Coloring field in my Dogs table to the Color ID field in my Coloring table, so I'm going to click on the Coloring field in the Dogs table.

6. Hold down the mouse button and drag away from the selected field. Your mouse pointer will turn into a little rectangle. Drop the little rectangle onto the destination field. For instance, I'm dragging to the Color ID field in the Coloring table. The Relationships dialog box appears (see Figure 25.3).

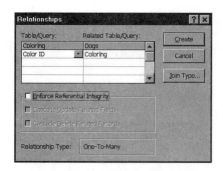

FIGURE 25.3   The Relationships dialog box asks you to define the relationship you're creating.

7. Choose any Referential Integrity options (see the following section), then click Create. A relationship will be created, and you'll see a line between the two fields in the Relationships window (see Figure 25.4).

You won't get the Infinity and 1 symbols on this line if you didn't choose Enforce Referential Integrity.

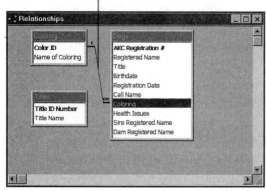

FIGURE 25.4   The line represents a relationship between the two fields.

Relationship Symbols Notice in Figure 25.4 that next to the Dogs table there's an infinity sign (looks like a sideways 8), and next to the Coloring table there's a 1. These symbols appear in relationships where Enforce Referential Integrity is turned on. The infinity sign means "many"—that means many records in this table can match a single record (hence the 1 sign) in the related Coloring table.

WHAT IS REFERENTIAL INTEGRITY?

Referential Integrity keeps you from making data entry mistakes. It says, essentially, that all the information in the two fields should match.

An example will make this clearer. In the Coloring field in my Dogs database, I have a number that matches up with the Color ID field in the Coloring table. The Coloring table lists all the allowable colors for the breed of dog. I don't want my clerks to be able to accidentally enter a number in the Dogs table that doesn't match up with any of the colors in the Coloring table, so I chose to Enforce Referential Integrity. Now Access won't let anyone enter anything in the Coloring field of the Dogs table (the "many" or infinity side) except one of the numbers contained in the Color ID field in the Coloring table (the one side).

What happens if someone tries? It depends on which of the other two check boxes shown in Figure 25.3 were marked.

Here is a summary of the check boxes:

- **Neither marked:** Access gives an error message that you need a related record in the "[Table Name]" and won't let you make the entry.

- **Cascade Update Related Fields:** If this check box is marked, and you make a change to the related table (in our example, the Coloring table), the change will be made in the other table too (the Dogs table). For instance, if I decided to change a certain coloring number from 7 to

8, and I made the change in the Coloring table (the one side), all the 7s in the Dog table (the many side) would change to 8s.

- **Cascade Delete Related Fields:** If this check box is marked, and you make a change to the "one" table (for instance, Coloring) so that the entries in the related table aren't valid anymore, Access will delete the entries in the related table. For instance, if I deleted the record in the Coloring table for Coloring ID number 3, all the dogs from my Dogs table that had coloring number 3 would also be deleted.

If you try to use Referential Integrity, you will likely get an error message the first time you try, because there is usually some condition that prevents it from working (as Murphy's Law goes). For instance, when I first created the relationship shown in Figure 25.4, with Enforce Referential Integrity marked, Access wouldn't allow it because the field type for the Coloring field in the Dogs table was set to Text while the Color ID field in the Coloring table was a number. (It didn't matter that I had entered only numbers in the Coloring field in the Dogs table.)

EDITING A RELATIONSHIP

Once a relationship is created, you can edit it by redisplaying the Relationships dialog box (refer to Figure 25.3). To do so, double-click the relationship's line. From there, you can edit the relationship using the same controls as you did when you created it.

REMOVING A RELATIONSHIP

To delete a relationship, just click on it in the Relationships window, then press the Delete key. Access will ask for confirmation; click Yes, and the relationship disappears.

In this lesson, you learned how to create, edit, and delete relationships between tables. In the next lesson, you will learn to analyze your database and find ways to improve its efficiency.

ANALYZING HOW WELL YOUR DATABASE WORKS

In this lesson, you'll learn about some new tools that come with Access 97 and can help you improve your database.

INTRODUCING THE ANALYSIS TOOLS

Have you ever wished for an expert to come along and take a look at your work to offer suggestions for improvement? That's the concept behind the analysis tools in Access. They include:

- **Table Analyzer Wizard** Analyzes your table, and splits it into related tables if needed.

- **Performance Analyzer** Checks any object (or multiple objects) in your database that you specify, and recommends suggestions for improving the object. You can implement most suggestions by just clicking a button.

- **Documenter** Provides detailed information about any or all objects in the database.

If you are wondering whether you have too much information in a table, or if you are sure you want to split a table, use the Table Analyzer. If you are just looking for general hints and suggestions, use the Performance Analyzer. (The Performance Analyzer can examine all objects, including tables.) If you need to keep notes on your database (for example, to provide to a programmer who will be setting up a custom application for your database), use the Documenter.

USING THE TABLE ANALYZER WIZARD

Follow these steps to use the Table Analyzer Wizard.

1. Select Tools, Analyze, Table. An introductory screen appears explaining what will be done.

2. Click Next > to continue. More explanations appear. Read them, then click Next > again, and the screen shown in Figure 26.1 appears.

A Quicker Start   In Figure 26.1, you see a check box called Show introductory pages? You can bypass the explanation screens the next time by clicking this check box now and removing the check mark.

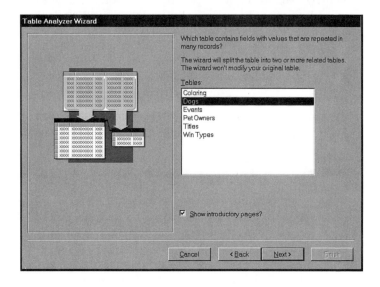

FIGURE 26.1   The first thing Access needs to know is which table to analyze.

3. Choose which table you want to analyze, then click Next >.

4. When asked if you want the wizard to decide which fields go in which tables, select Yes. That's what you want—the wizard's opinion. Then click Next >.

You're Good Already   After the wizard does its calculations, you may see a dialog box telling you that the Wizard recommends not splitting the table. If that happens, click Cancel and you're done.

5. The wizard presents you with its recommendations for splitting your table (see Figure 26.2). If you want to modify the recommendations, you can:

   • Create a new table by dragging fields out of one of the existing tables.

   • Drag fields between tables.

   • Rename a table from its generic name (Table1, and so on.) by selecting it, then clicking the Rename Table button (shown in Figure 26.2). If you don't do this, you'll see a warning message when you click Next reminding you to rename.

The Wizard Isn't Always Right   Sometimes the wizard will make suggestions for splitting a table that don't make sense. Make sure you pay close attention to the recommendations.

6. Click the Next > button to move on. Next you see a screen that looks a lot like Figure 26.2, except now it's asking about the Primary Key fields.

7. Make sure each table has a primary key field. They appear in bold on the field lists. Set one for each table that doesn't already show one by highlighting the field and clicking the key icon in the dialog box. Then click Next > to move on.

The wizard pulled out these fields into a separate table.

Select a new name then click the Rename button.

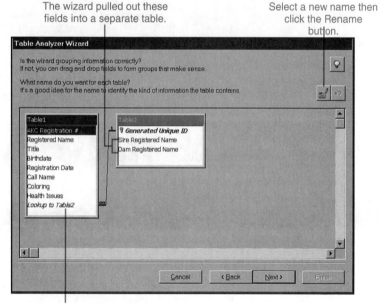

The wizard added a field in this table to connect the two tables.

FIGURE 26.2   The wizard's recommendations are shown in a window resembling the Relationships window.

8. If you have some records with very similar values, Access lists them and prompts you to make corrections. Do so if needed, then click Next.

9. Finally, you're asked if you want to create a query that works like the old table. Select Yes, create the query then click Finish.

10. A Help screen appears explaining the split table; read it and then close the Help window.

When you look on your Tables tab in your database, you now see the new tables that were created. You also see a table with the name of the original table plus _OLD. For instance, mine says Dogs_OLD. This is the query, disguised as a table; it enables you to use the old table just as you always have.

USING THE PERFORMANCE ANALYZER

The Performance Analyzer can check out your entire database, not just a single table. It lets you know what you could be doing to improve the efficiency and soundness of your database. You can choose to have it analyze a single object, or many objects.

Follow these steps:

1. Select Tools, Analyze, Performance. The Performance Analyzer dialog box appears (see Figure 26.3).

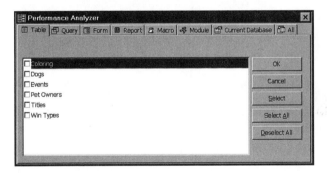

FIGURE 26.3   You can choose which objects you want to analyze.

2. Click on the tab for the object type you want to select, or click the All tab to see all the objects at the same time. Then click the check boxes on the tab to select the one you want to analyze.

3. Repeat step 2 until you've selected everything you want to analyze. For this example, I'm going to click the All tab, and then click the Select All button, to select every object in my database.

4. Click OK. The Performance Analyzer begins its analysis. Eventually a screen will appear like the one in Figure 26.4, reporting the findings.

You May Be Perfect Already   If you get a message that there are no suggestions for improvement, give yourself a pat on the back and click Close.

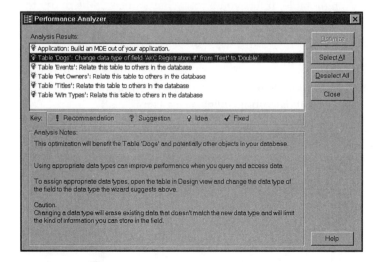

FIGURE 26.4   The Performance Analyzer shares suggestions for improvement.

5. Evaluate the ideas listed. When you see one you would like to execute, click it, then click the Optimize button.

Lightbulbs Are Ideas   The suggestions with the lightbulb symbol beside them are not automatically executable; they're merely ideas for you to keep in mind.

6. Depending on the change, you may be asked for input. For instance, I was asked to input a name for a new query that was being created. Do whatever is asked of you. When Access is done with the improvement, it will show a check mark next to it on the list.

7. Repeat steps 5 and 6 to implement all the suggestions you want, then click Close to exit.

USING THE DOCUMENTER

Generally, only database programmers have to know every little specification of a database, from the number of queries it contains to the number of characters in each field of a table. However, ordinary users occasionally have to know specific information like this too, to troubleshoot problems.

The Documenter provides all the nitty-gritty details about each object in your database in a handy, ready-to-print report format. To use it, follow these steps:

1. Select Tools, Analyze, Documenter. The Documenter dialog box appears (See Figure 26.5).

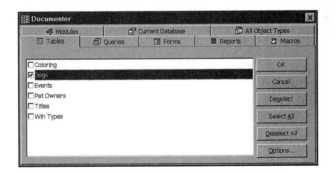

FIGURE 26.5 The Documenter dialog box enables you to select which components in your table you want information about.

2. Click on the tab for the type of object you want to select (for instance, Tables). Or, click the All Object Types tab to see all objects in one pane.

3. Click to place a check mark beside each object you want to document. You can select as many or as few objects as you want.

4. (Optional) To specify which information Access will provide about an object, select the object from the list, then click the Options button to display the Print Definition dialog box and choose the level of detail you want. For example, for a table you might choose to exclude information about relationships from the report by deselecting the Relationships check box. The options are different for each object type. When you're finished, click OK to return to the Documenter dialog box.

5. Click OK to generate the report. It appears in Print Preview, the same as any other report (for more information, see Lesson 21); you can read it or print it from there.

In this lesson, you learned how to analyze the effectiveness of your database and create a report containing database details. In the next lesson, you will learn about the tools that Access provides for Internet use.

USING ACCESS ON THE INTERNET

In this lesson, you will learn how to take advantage of Access 97's new Internet capabilities to link your work to the Internet.

SOME INTERNET BASICS

The Internet is a vast collection of connected computer networks, and the most popular component of it is the World Wide Web. Most Web files are stored in a format called Hypertext Markup Language, or HTML.

Access provides two ways to interact with the Internet—incoming and outgoing. In other words, you can provide Access information to people who use the Internet, or you can provide Internet information to people who use your Access database.

To provide information to incoming users (that is, visitors to your Web site), you can make parts of your database available by saving tables in HTML format and copying the files to an Internet host (a computer that's directly connected to the Internet). If your company provides an Internet connection through its LAN, it probably also has a host computer where you can save HTML files somewhere on the network. If you use a modem to connect to the Internet, the local host that you dial into may provide space on its server for your HTML files.

You can also set up hyperlinks to other URLs within a database, so that your database users can have outgoing access to Web sites. When your user clicks on a hyperlink as he is using the database, his Web browser program opens in a separate window and the specified URL is displayed.

Uniform Resource Locator (URL)   A URL is a Web address. It's like a phone number for the Internet. Most URLs begin with http://, followed by the site's name—for instance, **http://www.mcp.com**. Some URLs also contain specific directory and file names, like this: **http://www.mcp.com/Pub/index.htm**. Pub/ is a directory, and index.htm is a file name.

Hyperlink   A hyperlink is a bit of text or a picture that you can click to access a specific URL quickly. When you click on a hyperlink, your Web browser program opens (if you have one set up) and the specified URL's data is displayed.

Publish to the Web

Access provides a quick way to save many objects at a time in HTML format: The Publish to the Web option. It lets you simultaneously select multiple objects for saving to your local hard disk. There is also an option for saving them directly to the server. If your server is using Microsoft software (Microsoft Web Server or Personal Web Server), you can even use the Publish to the Web Wizard to set up dynamic links to your Access database, so that the person accessing it from the Internet or intranet always sees the most recent data.

Follow these steps to check it out:

1. Open the database containing the objects you want to publish.

2. Select File, Save As HTML. The Publish to the Web wizard opens.

3. Read the introductory information, and then click Next > to continue.

4. Select which objects you want to publish (see Figure 27.1). There is a separate tab for each object type. Then click Next > to continue.

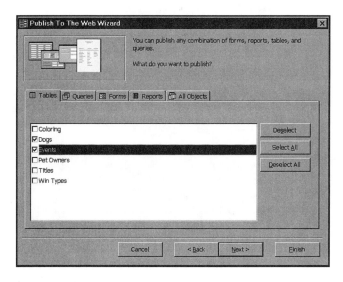

FIGURE 27.1   Place a check mark beside each object you want
to publish on the Web.

5. Next you're asked about templates. If there is another
   HTML file that you want to use as a template for the ones
   you are now creating, type its path in the text box, or
   click the Browse button to locate it. Or, to use different
   templates for different pages, click the check box below
   the options. Then click Next >.

6. If you clicked the check box in step 5, an extra screen
   appears asking you to specify which templates go with
   which documents. Select specific objects from the list,
   and then click the Browse button to find the HTML file to
   use as a template for them. When you're finished choosing templates, click Next > to move on.

7. Next you're asked whether you want static (HTML) or
   dynamic (HTX/IDC or ASP) pages. Dynamic pages are
   updated automatically when your Access database is updated, but require your server to be running Microsoft
   server software. Static pages are ordinary exported HTML
   files. Choose one or the other, or click the check box below the options to indicate you want some of each type.

8. If you selected the check box in step 7, an extra screen appears (see Figure 27.2) in which you must specify which pages should be static and which dynamic. Click an object on the list, then click the HTML, HTX/IDC, or ASP option button to choose its status. (HTML is static; the other two are dynamic formats.) Repeat for all objects on the list, and then click Next > to move on.

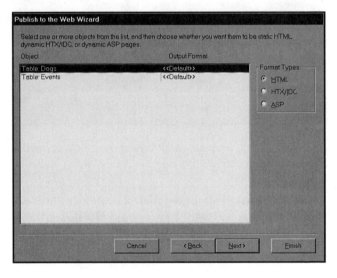

FIGURE 27.2 You can specify which pages should be static and which should be dynamic in this dialog box.

TIP **Use Dynamic Sparingly**   Dynamic pages will take longer for a user to access than static ones, because the server has to check your Access database. If you do not anticipate the information for a particular object changing frequently, it's better to save it as a static page.

9. If you chose Dynamic for any of your pages, a screen appears asking you for information about the server—its Data Source Name name and, optionally, the user name and password you use to connect to it. You can also enter

ActiveX Server Output information here. Enter the information, then click Next.

10. Next you're asked about storage. By default, all HTML files will be saved on your hard disk. Specify the drive and folder in the text box labeled I Want to Put My Web Documents in this Folder.

11. If you want the HTML files saved on a server too (in addition to the copy kept on your hard drive), click one of the Yes buttons at the bottom of the dialog box. (They are not available if you are not currently connected to your server.) They are:

- **Yes, I want to run the Web Publishing Wizard to set up a new Web Publishing Specification.** Use this one the first time, to set up the information for your server. If you choose this, the Web Publishing Wizard starts and you must work through its series of dialog boxes and supply the needed information.

Server Info?   If you are not sure about your server information, ask your system administrator or service provider. Don't try to guess about this information.

- **Yes, I want to use an existing Web Publishing Server whose 'friendly name' has been set up previously.** Use this after you have already set up your server's information, to use the same server that you used last time. Select your server's Friendly Name from the drop-down list.

Friendly Name   When you use the Web Publishing Wizard to set up your server's information, you're prompted to enter a Friendly Name for it. This is simply a plain-English name that you can readily identify with that server. For instance, I might call the Macmillan Publishing server "Macmillan."

12. Click Next > to move on when you're finished specifying the storage locations.

13. Next you're asked whether you want to create a home page. If you select the **Yes, I want to create a home page** check box, a home page HTML file will be added to the storage location(s) you specified in step 10.

14. If you marked the check box in step 13, enter a title for the page in the What file name...text box. This is the name the file will be saved as (for example, Default.htm). This file will contain hyperlinks to all the other objects' pages you're creating. Then click Next >.

15. Next, you're asked whether you want to save your wizard answers in a Web Publication profile. Click Yes and enter the profile name or click No.

16. Click Finish. Access generates the HTML files you specified and posts them to the location(s) you selected.

INSERTING HYPERLINKS INTO AN ACCESS OBJECT

There are two ways to add a hyperlink to an Access database. The first is to create a field in a table and set its Data Type as Hyperlink. Then any text that you enter into that field becomes a hyperlink that you can click to open a specified Web page. For instance, in Figure 27.3 I'm setting up a Breeders Home Page field in my Dogs table, to hold the URLs for the home pages of the breeders from which I bought my dogs. Then, as you can see in Figure 27.4, I can enter URLs into that field that immediately become underlined hyperlinks.

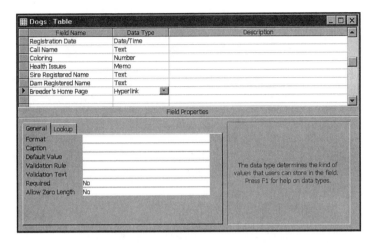

FIGURE 27.3   By setting the Data Type to Hyperlink, I'm telling
Access that any data entered in this field is a URL.

Hyperlink

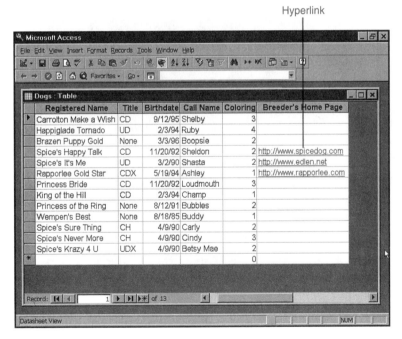

FIGURE 27.4   Any data entered into a field with a Hyperlink data
type becomes a hyperlink.

> **Not for Web Use Only**   You can hyperlink to a docu-
> ment on your hard disk or on your LAN instead of a Web
> address, if you like. For instance, if you have a supporting
> document for a record (such as a contract in Word for
> Windows), you can enter the path to the document in a
> hyperlink field (for instance, c:\mydocuments\contract1.
> doc).

The other way to set up a hyperlink is to add it to a form or report. This way, it's not associated with any particular record, but
rather with the entire form or table. To do this:

1. Open the form or report in Design view.

2. Click the Insert Hyperlink button on the toolbar. The
   Insert Hyperlink dialog box appears (Figure 27.5).

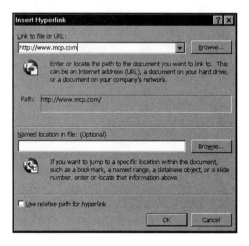

Figure 27.5   Specify the URL for the hyperlink in the Insert
Hyperlink dialog box.

3. Enter the file or URL to hyperlink to in the Link to File or
   URL text box.

4. Click OK. Access inserts the hyperlink in the active section. You can drag it to move it to any position on the

form you like, just as you can move any object on a form (see Lesson 14).

The previous method inserts a simple text hyperlink that lists the URL. If you want something fancier, you can create a picture and assign the hyperlink to it. Follow these steps to create a picture that serves as a hyperlink:

1. Insert a picture in the report or form, as you learned to do in Lesson 16.

2. Right-click on the picture and select Properties from the shortcut menu that appears.

3. In the Properties box, click the Format tab.

4. Type the URL in the Hyperlink Address text box (see Figure 27.6).

5. Close the Properties box. Now when you click on the picture, it activates the hyperlink.

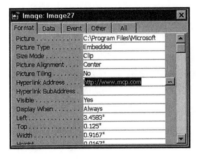

FIGURE 27.6   Specify a URL address in the Hyperlink Address text box and the picture becomes a hyperlinked object.

In this lesson, you learned how to connect your Access data with the World Wide Web. In the next lesson, you will learn how to keep your data safe from various perils, such as system crashes, viruses, and intruders.

KEEPING YOUR DATA SAFE

In this lesson, you'll learn several perils and how to protect against them.

DATA SECURITY: WHAT TO BE AFRAID OF

It's not paranoid to be protective of your data. Whether it's your home financial records or your company's account data, you're right to be concerned about its safety. In this lesson, we'll take a look at several ways you can lose or corrupt data, and learn how to prevent it.

SETTING UP EXCLUSIVE USE

You can't set a password for a database (see the following section) if the database is open in Shared mode. Shared mode lets more than one person work on a database at once on a network.

By default, databases are opened in Shared mode. You can override this, and open a database in Exclusive mode, by selecting the **Exclusive** check box in the Open dialog box when you open the file.

If you want to set the default to Exclusive mode for all databases you open, follow these steps:

1. Select Tools, Options. The Options dialog box appears.

2. Click the Advanced tab.

3. In the Default Open Mode area, click Exclusive.

4. Click OK.

Why Isn't It Exclusive? If you are reopening your database after you've set the default for Exclusive (see the steps above), use the File, Open command. Don't pick the database from the bottom of the File menu. Why? When you open it from its name on the File menu, it opens with the same options it opened with before. If it wasn't in Exclusive mode before, it won't be now.

ASSIGNING PASSWORDS TO DATABASE FILES

The easiest way to prevent other people from making changes to your database is to assign a password to it. Anyone who doesn't know the password will be prevented from opening the file. You must have the database open in Exclusive mode (see the preceding section) in order to set a password for it.

SETTING A PASSWORD

Follow these steps to set a database password:

1. Open the database that you want to protect.

2. Select Tools, Security, Set Database Password. The Set Database Password dialog box appears.

3. Enter the password you want to use in the Password text box, then enter it again in the Verify text box (see Figure 28.1). Click OK.

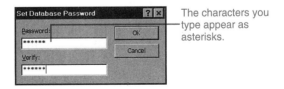

The characters you type appear as asterisks.

FIGURE 28.1   Enter your password twice, to make sure you've typed it correctly.

The next time you try to open the database, a dialog box will appear asking for the password. Type it and click OK.

REMOVING OR CHANGING A PASSWORD

Changing the password is a two-phase process: First you remove the old password and then you set a new one. Follow these steps to remove the old one, and then follow the previous procedure to set a new one.

To remove a password:

1. Open the database.

2. Select Tools, Security, Unset Database Password. A dialog box appears asking for the current password.

3. Type the current password, then click OK. The password is now gone from the database.

USER-LEVEL SECURITY (NETWORK ONLY)

Access is designed for group use, so it has some powerful features that let you control the access to the database by users or groups. These features aren't useful for stand-alone computers; you have to be on a network.

You can use Tools, Security, User and Group Accounts to create profiles for users and groups, and then Tools, Security, User and Group Permissions to give permissions for each object in the open database. See your network administrator for help if needed.

There's also a User-Level Security Wizard you can follow. This Wizard creates a secured database that is a duplicate of your original and helps you set up permissions for it for your workgroup. To use it, just select Tools, Security, User-Level Security Wizard and follow the prompts.

CREATING AN MDE FILE

When your intended end-user enters data into your database file, or views information with a query you created, or prints a report with a report you designed, she does not need access to the controls you used to create those objects. All she needs is access to the objects themselves. In fact, it's probably better that your end users do not have access to the Design views for your objects because the integrity of your database will be maintained. When you create an MDE file from your database file, you're creating a streamlined version of the database. It's the same as the original, but there is no access to the design controls. Users of an MDE file can use all your forms, tables, and so on, but they cannot view and modify them in Design view. You also cannot create new forms or reports. This is not only handy from a security standpoint, but it also makes the database more efficient, so it works smoother and quicker.

 You Can't Go Back! Be very sure that the database objects' structures are exactly the way you want them before you create an MDE file. If you need to modify the design of forms, reports, or tables in a database saved as an MDE file, you must open the original database, make the changes, and then save it as an MDE file again. Any data entry you've done in the original MDE file must be duplicated in the new MDE file, which can be a significant amount of work.

To save a database file as an MDE file, follow these steps:

1. Open the database you want to save as an MDE file.

2. Select Tools, Database Utilities, Make MDE File. The Save MDE As dialog box appears. (It's just like a regular Save As dialog box.)

3. Enter the name you want to use for the MDE file in the File Name text box, and then click Make MDE File.

To open and use an MDE file, use the same procedure you learned for opening database files in Lesson 6 (**File, Open**) except change the Files of Type drop-down list to MDE Files (***.mde**).

ENCRYPTING A DATABASE

Encryption "scrambles" the contents of a database so it's indecipherable, even by a utility program that an expert user might employ to see your database from outside of Access. If you are worried that password protection is not enough security, you might encrypt the database as well as password-protect it. You must decrypt it before you can use it again.

 Only the Owner If you are working in a shared file environment, such as a network, you may have access to files that you are not the owner of. Only the owner can encrypt a database file.

To encrypt a database, follow these steps:

1. Close all databases. This is important; you can't encrypt a database that is open.

2. Select Tools, Security, Encrypt/Database.

3. In the Encrypt/Decrypt Database dialog box, choose the database file you want to encrypt. (This looks and works just like the Open dialog box.) Click OK.

4. In the Encrypt As dialog box, type a new name for the encrypted file. The original copy will be untouched. (This looks and works just like the Save As dialog box.) Click Save.

Encrypting creates a new copy of the database, but the old, unsecure version still remains. After encrypting, you will want to use Windows Explorer to find and delete the original database file on which the encrypted copy was based.

To decrypt the database, repeat the process. In step 2 you will choose Tools, Security, Decrypt this time. In step 4, the dialog box will be called Decrypt As, but the procedure is identical.

DATA PROTECTION ON FORMS

You can protect individual fields on a form from changes if you like. For instance, I might protect the AKC Registration # field in my Kennel database from changes, so I don't accidentally over-write these important numbers.

To protect a field on a form:

1. Open the form in Form Design view.

2. Right-click on the field and select Properties.

3. Click on the Data tab.

4. Change the Locked property to Yes (see Figure 28.2).

5. Close the Properties box.

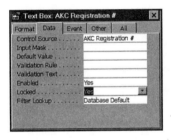

FIGURE 28.2   Protect an individual field on a form by locking it.

You can protect an entire form from changes, making it "read-only." For instance, if you kept your company's work schedule on a form that employees could access, you would want to keep un-happy employees from changing their work hours. To do so:

1. Open the form in Form Design view.

2. Click in the square at the intersection of the two rulers (in the top-left corner) to select the entire form (shown in Figure 28.3).

3. Select View, Properties.

4. Select the Data tab. To prevent changes to existing records, set Allow Editing to No (see Figure 28.3).

Click here to select the entire form.

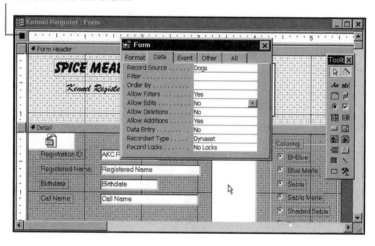

FIGURE 28.3   Control editing for the entire form from here.

5. To prevent deletions of existing records, set Allow Deletions to No.

6. To prevent additional records, set Allow Additions to No.

7. Close the Properties box.

BACKING UP YOUR DATA

There are several ways to back up your data to another disk:

- Copy the database file to a floppy disk. Make sure you copy both the main database file (ends in .MDB) and the associated file (ends in .LDB). You should also back up System.MDW, the workgroup information file.

Make a duplicate of the database by saving it under a different file name. Use the File, Save As/Export command.

- Back up your database file using the Backup program that comes with Windows 95. It's located in the Programs/Accessories/System Tools folder on the Start menu. If it's not there, use the Add/Remove Programs utility in the Control Panel to add it. (You will need your original Windows 95 diskettes or CD handy.)

Just One Table   If you just want to back up a single table (or other object), import it to a new, empty database, and then back up only the new database.

REPAIRING DAMAGED DATABASE FILES

In most cases, when you try to work with a damaged database, Access will detect it and offer to repair the database. But if your database is damaged and Access does not detect it, follow these steps to repair it:

1. Close all databases.

2. Select Tools, Database Utilities, Repair Database.

3. Select the database you want to repair, then click Repair. Access repairs it.

After you run Repair you should always run Compact. Compacting makes a copy of your database and leaves the original. Compacting also rearranges how the database file is stored to make better use of disk space. To Compact a database, open the database and select Tools, Database Utilities, Compact Database. The compacting process is totally automatic; no other action is required.

In this lesson, you learned many ways to protect your database. In the next lesson, you will learn how to import and export data.

LESSON 29

IMPORTING AND EXPORTING DATA

In this lesson, you'll learn several ways to share Access data with other programs.

WHY SHARE DATA?

Access is a great program as a stand-alone, but sometimes you may need to use an Access table in another program. For instance, maybe your boss wants a copy of a mailing list so he can make some cuts in it, but he's a die-hard Excel user with no interest in learning Access. You can give him the table in Excel format, and then when he's finished with it, you can import it back into an Access table.

Or perhaps you have used a different database program, like dBase or FoxPro, and now you want to convert your databases over to Access. You can import the data, and save it in Access format.

IMPORTING DATA FROM OTHER PROGRAMS

Access accepts data from a wide variety of database programs, making it very easy to switch to Access without much loss of pro-ductivity. To import data from another program, follow these steps:

1. Open the Access database into which you want to import the data. You may want to create a new, empty database especially for this purpose (see Lesson 5).

2. Select File, Get External Data, Import. The Import dialog box opens (see Figure 29.1).

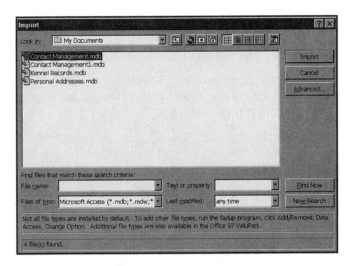

FIGURE 29.1   You can import data from a variety of sources.

3. Open the Files of type drop-down list and select the type of file the data is coming from. If the type you want is not listed, rerun the Microsoft Office setup program and choose Custom installation, and install the import/export filter you need.

4. Change the drive or folder to the one where the file is stored. The file's name appears in the list box in the middle of the dialog box.

 It's Not There   If the file name does not appear in the list box, either you are in the wrong folder or drive, or you have selected the wrong file type.

5. Double-click the file name, or click it and then click Import.

A variety of things might happen next, depending on what type of file you're importing from. See the following sections.

IMPORTING FROM A DATABASE PROGRAM

All the database programs that Access supports imports from (FoxPro, Paradox, and dBase) have file formats that are similar enough to Access that there's no fuss.

After you click on Import (step 5 in the previous procedure), Access takes a moment, then displays a message like **Successfully imported file name**. That's all there is to it; the imported table appears on the Tables tab of your database.

IMPORTING FROM A SPREADSHEET

If you followed the preceding procedure for a spreadsheet file, the Import Spreadsheet Wizard opens next, as shown in Figure 29.2.

Follow these steps to finish the import:

1. At the first Import Spreadsheet Wizard screen, click on the worksheet you want to import, if there is more than one. (There is only one in Figure 29.2.) A sample of it appears in the dialog box. Then click Next >.

2. If the first row contains your field names, click the First Row Contains Column Headings check box. Click Next > to continue.

3. Next you choose where you want to store your data: **In a New Table** or **In an Existing Table**. If you select **In an Existing Table**, select the table from the drop-down list. Then click Next >.

4. Next you can choose the names for the fields you're importing (see Figure 29.3). For the first field name, type a different title in the Field Name box if you like, and select Yes or No from the Indexed drop-down list. If you don't want that field at all in the imported table, select the Do Not Import Field (Skip) check box.

Click the worksheet you want to import as a table.

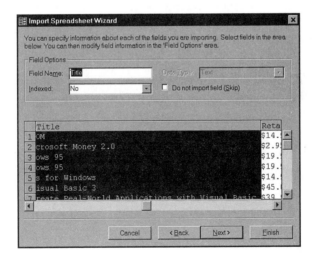

FIGURE 29.2   The Import Spreadsheet Wizard guides you through.

FIGURE 29.3   You can change field names if you like.

5. Use the horizontal scroll bar in at the bottom of the dialog box to move the next field into view, and then click

on it. Then repeat step 4. Go through all the fields this
way, and then click Next > to continue.

6. Next you're asked to make a Primary Key field. If your
spreadsheet has a unique column that you want to use as
a primary key, click Choose my own Primary Key and
select it from the drop-down list. Otherwise, click Let
Access Add Primary Key. Click Next > to continue.

7. Next you're asked for a name for the table. Enter one,
then click Finish. Access imports the spreadsheet into
your current database as a table.

8. Click OK at the confirmation message box to clear it. You
can now see your imported table on the Tables tab of the
Database window.

IMPORTING FROM A TEXT FILE

If you're importing data from a text file, that's fine, as long as the
fields and records are delimited in some way. In other words,
there has to be some commonly-used separator characters to show
where one field ends and the next one begins, and where one
record ends and the next record begins.

In most database text files, a hard return (made by pressing the
Enter key) marks the end of a record. Each record is on its own
line, then. The fields of individual records are usually marked
with either tabs or commas.

Delimited   Delimited means separated, basically. A tab-
delimited database's fields are separated by tab stops; a
comma-delimited database's fields are separated by
commas.

If you're importing data from a text file, you'll need to follow the
steps at the beginning of this lesson under the heading "Importing Data from Other Programs." The Import Text Wizard opens
and you can follow these steps:

1. On the first screen of the Import Text Wizard, choose Delimited if your text file has delimiters like commas or tabs that separate each field. If not, you'll have to rely on spacing—choose Fixed Width. Click Next to continue.

 Fixed Width   This option is for text files where the fields were set into columns by pressing the space bar. For instance, if each field were 20 spaces wide, and a particular record's entry in that field took 10 characters, there would be 10 spaces before the next field's entry.

2. If you chose Delimited, you're asked to choose the delimiter character. Your choices are **Tab, Semicolon, Comma, Space**, or **Other**. In the Other text box, you can type in any character.

3. If the first row contains your field names, select the First Row Contains Field Names check box.

4. Click Next to continue.

5. Next you're asked where you want information to be stored: in a new table or an existing one. Click the In a new table button, or click the In an existing table button and then select the table from the drop-down list. Click Next to continue.

6. In the Field Options box, you can change the field names for each field if you like. Enter your preferences, then click Next.

7. To allow Access to create a new primary key field, click Let Access add Primary Key. Or specify one of the existing fields as the primary key if you prefer, or select No Primary Key. Click Next.

8. Enter a name to save the table under, then click Finish. The table appears on your Tables tab.

EXPORTING DATA TO OTHER PROGRAMS

You cannot export an entire Access database to another program. That's because Access uses all kinds of special organizing methods, like Tables, Forms, Queries, Reports, and Macros, and these wouldn't translate easily into another program.

Besides, if you want to export data, what you really want to export is a table. Tables in Access contain all your data.

Follow these steps to export a table:

1. Open the database that contains the table.

2. Click on the Tables tab, and highlight the database you want to export.

3. Select File, Save As/Export. The Save As dialog box appears (Figure 29.4).

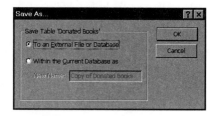

FIGURE 29.4   Export your table by saving it in a different format.

4. Click To an External File or Database, then click OK. The Save Table (Table Name) In dialog box appears. (The exact name of the dialog box will depend on the table name.)

5. If desired, choose a different drive or folder.

6. Open the Save as Type drop-down list and choose the file type you want.

7. Type a name in the File Name text box to create a new file to save it in, or choose one of the existing files from the list above it. If you save a table in an existing Access database file, it becomes another table among the tables in that file.

8. Open the Save as type drop-down list and choose the format into which you want to save.

9. Click the Export button. Access saves the table in the specified format.

CREATING OLE LINKS

If you want to import a file that might change later, you might be better off creating a dynamic link to that file than importing it outright. With a link in place, if the file changes later, the changes will be reflected in the file imported into Access.

It's Slower Don't use this procedure unless you are sure you need a link, rather than a simple import. Having a link in your database slows Access down when it opens a file.

Follow these steps to create a table in Access that's linked to an external file:

1. Select File, Get External Data, Link Tables. The Link dialog box appears.

2. Change the drive or folder if necessary.

3. Select the file type from the Files of type drop-down list.

4. Double-click the file name to open the file or select the file and click the Link button.

5. With some types of database files, you'll be asked to choose an Index file. Choose one if you have one; otherwise click Cancel to exit that dialog box.

6. If you're importing a spreadsheet or text file, you'll go through the respective Wizard for that file type, as you learned earlier in the lesson.

7. When you get a message saying the task is complete, click OK.

When the import is complete, look on the Tables tab. You'll see your linked file, with an icon (representing the type of type you are linked to) and a right arrow beside it, indicating the link.

In this lesson, you learned to import and export data.